MAC_____ER GUIDES

THE TEMPEST

BY WILLIAM SHAKESPEARE

KENNETH PICKERING

with an Introduction by
HAROLD BROOKS

D0264141

MACMILLAN

First published 1986 by
MACMILLAN PRESS LTD
Houndmills, Basingstoke, Hampshire RG21 6XS
and London
Companies and representatives
throughout the world

ISBN 0–333–40260–X

A catalogue record for this book is available
from the British Library.

11 10   9   8   7   6   5   4
04 03 02 01 00 99 98

Printed in Hong Kong

CONTENTS

ACKNOWLEDGEMENTS

I am pleased to acknowledge the help and encouragement of Dr James
Gibson, Mr Keith Cole and my wife, Irene Pickering, in the preparation of
this book.

Cover illustration: *Dutch ships running on to a rocky coast* by A. van Ertvelt,
© National Maritime Museum.

NOTE: It is important to use a good modern edition of the play which
has the benefits of recent scholarship. The recommended edition to which
all references will apply in this guide is *The Tempest* edited by A. C. and
J. E. Spearing in *The Macmillan Shakespeare*. This contains a particularly
helpful introduction. The Arden Edition, edited by Frank Kermode, will
be found invaluable.

KENNETH PICKERING

GENERAL EDITOR'S PREFACE

The aim of the Macmillan Master Guides is to help you to appreciate the book you are studying by providing information about it and by suggesting ways of reading and thinking about it which will lead to a fuller understanding. The section on the writer's life and background has been designed to illustrate those aspects of the writer's life which have influenced the work, and to place it in its personal and literary context. The summaries and critical commentary are of special importance in that each brief summary of the action is followed by an examination of the significant critical points. The space which might have been given to repetitive explanatory notes has been devoted to a detailed analysis of the kind of passage which might confront you in an examination. Literary criticism is concerned with both the broader aspects of the work being studied and with its detail. The ideas which meet us in reading a great work of literature, and their relevance to us today, are an essential part of our study, and our Guides look at the thought of their subject in some detail. But just as essential is the craft with which the writer has constructed his work of art, and this may be considered under several technical headings – characterisation, language, style and stagecraft, for example.

The authors of these Guides are all teachers and writers of wide experience, and they have chosen to write about books they admire and know well in the belief that they can communicate their admiration to you. But you yourself must read and know intimately the book you are studying. No one can do that for you. You should see this book as a lamppost. Use it to shed light, not to lean against. If you know your text and know what it is saying about life, and how it says it, then you will enjoy it, and there is no better way of passing an examination in literature.

JAMES GIBSON

AN INTRODUCTION TO THE STUDY OF SHAKESPEARE'S PLAYS

A play as a work of art exists to the full only when performed. It must hold the audience's attention throughout the performance, and, unlike a novel, it can't be put down and taken up again. It is important to experience the play as if you are seeing it on the stage for the first time, and you should begin by reading it straight through. Shakespeare builds a play in dramatic units which may be divided into smaller subdivisions, or episodes, marked off by exits and entrances and lasting as long as the same actors are on the stage. Study it unit by unit.

The first unit provides the exposition which is designed to put the audience into the picture. In the second unit we see the forward movement of the play as one situation changes into another. The last unit in a tragedy or a tragical play will bring the catastrophe and in comedy – and some of the history plays – an unravelling of the complications, what is called a *dénouement*.

The onward movement of the play from start to finish is its progressive structure. We see the chain of cause and effect (the plot) and the progressive revelation and development of character. The people, their characters and their motives drive the plot forward in a series of scenes which are carefully planned to give variety of pace and excitement. We notice fast-moving and slower-moving episodes, tension mounting and slackening, and alternate fear and hope for the characters we favour. Full-stage scenes, such as stately councils and processions or turbulent mobs, contrast with scenes of small groups or even single speakers. Each of the scenes presents a deed or event which changes the situation. In performance, entrances and exits and stage actions are physical facts, with more impact than on the page. That impact Shakespeare relied upon, and we must restore it by an effort of the imagination.

Shakespeare's language is just as diverse. Quickfire dialogue is followed by long speeches, and verse changes to prose. There is a wide range of speech – formal, colloquial, dialect, 'Mummerset' and the broken English of foreigners, for example. Songs, instrumental music, and the noise of battle, revelry and tempest, all extend the range of dramatic expression. The dramatic use of language is enhanced by skilful stagecraft, by costumes, by properties such as beds, swords and Yorick's skull, by such stage business as kneeling, embracing and giving money, and by use of such features of the stage structure as the balcony and the trapdoor.

By these means Shakespeare's people are brought vividly to life and cleverly individualised. But though they have much to tell us about human nature, we must never forget that they are characters in a play, not in real life. And remember, they exist to enact the play, not the play to portray *them*.

Shakespeare groups his characters so that they form a pattern, and it is useful to draw a diagram showing this. Sometimes a linking character has dealings with each group. The pattern of persons belongs to the symmetric structure of the play, and its dramatic unity is reinforced and enriched by a pattern of resemblances and contrasts; for instance, between characters, scenes, recurrent kinds of imagery, and words. It is not enough just to notice a feature that belongs to the symmetric structure, you should ask what its relevance is to the play as a whole and to the play's ideas.

These ideas and the dramatising of them in a central theme, or several related to each other, are a principal source of the dramatic unity. In order to see what themes are present and important, look, as before, for pattern. Observe the place in it of the leading character. In tragedy this will be the protagonist, in comedy heroes and heroines, together with those in conflict or contrast with them. In *Henry IV Part I*, Prince Hal is being educated for kingship and has a correct estimate of honour, while Falstaff despises honour, and Hotspur makes an idol of it. Pick out the episodes of great intensity as, for example, in *King Lear* where the theme of spiritual blindness is objectified in the blinding of Gloucester, and, similarly, note the emphases given by dramatic poetry as in Prospero's 'Our revels now are ended . . . ' or unforgettable utterances such as Lear's 'Is there any cause in Nature that makes these hard hearts?' Striking stage-pictures such as that of Hamlet behind the King at prayer will point to leading themes, as will all the parallels and recurrences, including those of phrase and imagery. See whether, in the play you are studying, themes known to be favourites with Shakespeare are prominent, themes such as those of order and disorder, relationships disrupted by mistakes about identity, and appearance and reality. The latter were bound to fascinate Shakespeare, whose theatrical art worked by means of illusions which pointed beyond the surface of actual life to underlying truths. In looking at themes beware of attempts to make the play fit some orthodoxy a critic believes in – Freudian perhaps, or Marxist, or dogmatic Christian theology – and remember that its ideas, though they often have a bearing on ours, are Elizabethan.

Some of Shakespeare's greatness lies in the good parts he wrote for the actors. In his demands upon them, and the opportunities he provided, he bore their professional skills in mind and made use of their physical prowess, relished by a public accustomed to judge fencing and wrestling as expertly as we today judge football and tennis. As a member of the professional group of players called the Chamberlain's Men he knew each actor he was writing for. To play his women he had highly trained boys. As paired heroines they were often contrasted, short with tall, for example, or one vivacious and enterprising, the other more conventionally feminine.

Richard Burbage, the company's leading man, was famous as a great tragic actor, and he took leading roles in seven of Shakespeare's *tragedies*. Though each of the seven has its own distinctiveness, we shall find at the centre of all of them a tragic protagonist possessing tragic greatness, not just one 'tragic flaw' but a tragic vulnerability. He will have a character which makes him unfit to cope with the tragic situations confronting him, so that his tragic errors bring down upon him tragic suffering and finally a tragic catastrophe. Normally, both the suffering and the catastrophe are far worse than he can be said to deserve, and others are engulfed in them who deserve such a fate less or not at all. Tragic terror is aroused in us because, though exceptional, he is sufficiently near to normal humankind for his fate to remind us of what can happen to human beings like ourselves, and because we see in it a combination of inexorable law and painful mystery. We recognise the principle of cause and effect where in a tragic world errors return upon those who make them, but we are also aware of the tragic disproportion between cause and effect. In a tragic world you may kick a stone and start an avalanche which will destroy you and others with you. Tragic pity is aroused in us by this disproportionate suffering, and also by all the kinds of suffering undergone by every character who has won our imaginative sympathy. Imaginative sympathy is wider than moral approval, and is felt even if suffering does seem a just and logical outcome. In addition to pity and terror we have a sense of tragic waste because catastrophe has affected so much that was great and fine. Yet we feel also a tragic exaltation. To our grief the men and women who represented those values have been destroyed, but the values themselves have been shown not to depend upon success, nor upon immunity from the worst of tragic suffering and disaster.

Comedies have been of two main kinds, or cross-bred from the two. In critical comedies the governing aim is to bring out the absurdity or irrationality of follies and abuses, and make us laugh at them. Shakespeare's comedies often do this, but most of them belong primarily to the other kind – romantic comedy. Part of the romantic appeal is to our liking for suspense; they are dramas of averted threat, beginning in trouble and ending in joy. They appeal to the romantic senses of adventure and of wonder, and to complain that they are improbable is silly because the improbability, the marvellousness, is part of the pleasure. They dramatise stories of romantic love, accompanied by love doctrine – ideas and ideals of love. But they are plays in two tones, they are comic as well as romantic. There is often something to laugh at even in the love stories of the nobility and gentry, and just as there is high comedy in such incidents as the cross-purposes of the young Athenians in the wood, and Rosalind as 'Ganymede' teasing Orlando, there is always broad comedy for characters of lower rank. Even where one of the sub-plots has no effect on the main plot, it may take up a topic from it and present it in a more comic way.

What is there in the play to make us laugh or smile? We can distinguish many kinds of comedy it may employ. *Language* can amuse by its wit, or by absurdity, as in Bottom's malapropisms. Feste's nonsense-phrases, so fatuously admired by Sir Andrew, are deliberate, while his catechising of Olivia is clown-routine. Ass-headed Bottom embraced by the Fairy Queen is a *comic spectacle* combining costume and stage-business. His wanting to play every part is *comedy of character*. Phebe disdaining Silvius and in love with 'Ganymed', or Malvolio treating Olivia as though she had written him a love-letter is *comedy of situation*; the situation is laughably different from what Phebe or Malvolio supposes. A comic let-down or anticlimax can be devastating, as we see when Aragon, sure that he deserves Portia, chooses the silver casket only to find the portrait not of her but of a 'blinking idiot'. By *slapstick, caricature* or sheer *ridiculousness of situation*, comedy can be exaggerated into farce, which Shakespeare knows how to use on occasion. At the opposite extreme, before he averts the threat, he can carry it to the brink of tragedy, but always under control.

Dramatic irony is the result of a character or the audience anticipating an outcome which, comically or tragically, turns out very differently. Sometimes *we* foresee that it will. The speaker never foresees how ironical, looking back, the words or expectations will appear. When she says, 'A little water clears us of this deed' Lady Macbeth has no prevision of her sleep-walking words, 'Will these hands ne'er be clean?' There is irony in the way in which in all Shakespeare's tragic plays except *Richard II* comedy is found in the very heart of the tragedy. The Porter scene in *Macbeth* comes straight after Duncan's murder. In *Hamlet* and *Antony and Cleopatra* comic episodes lead into the catastrophe: the rustic Countryman brings Cleopatra the means of death, and the satirised Osric departs with Hamlet's assent to the fatal fencing match. The Porter, the Countryman and Osric are not mere 'comic relief', they contrast with the tragedy in a way that adds something to it, and affects our response.

A sense of the comic and the tragic is common ground between Shakespeare and his audience. Understandings shared with the audience are necessary to all drama. They include conventions, i.e. assumptions, contrary to what factual realism would demand, which the audience silently agrees to accept. It is, after all, by a convention, what Coleridge called a 'willing suspension of disbelief', that an actor is accepted as Hamlet. We should let a play teach us the conventions it depends on. Shakespeare's conventions allow him to take a good many liberties, and he never troubles about inconsistencies that wouldn't trouble an audience. What matters to the dramatist is the effect he creates. So long as we are responding as he would wish, Shakespeare would not care whether we could say by what means he has made us do so. But to appreciate his skill, and get a fuller understanding of his play, we have to distinguish these means, and find terms to describe them.

If you approach the Shakespeare play you are studying bearing in mind what is said to you here, then you will respond to it more fully than before. Yet like all works of artistic genius, Shakespeare's can only be analysed so far. His drama and its poetry will always have about them something 'which into words no critic can digest'.

HAROLD BROOKS

1 WILLIAM SHAKESPEARE: LIFE AND BACKGROUND

We know comparatively little about the life and career of Shakespeare and what we do know has to be pieced together from fragments of evidence. He spent much of his life involved in the theatre which (though not for the same reason) was probably as precarious an existence in Elizabethan times as it is today, and actors enjoyed little social standing and left few records. Playwrights and actors were too preoccupied with rehearsing, performing and preparing scripts for the next show to be over-concerned with the interest of posterity but such evidence as we have suggests that William Shakespeare was an unusually shrewd businessman and a very popular dramatist in his own lifetime.

He was born in Stratford-upon-Avon, Warwickshire, and baptised on 26 April 1564. At the time of his birth Shakespeare's father, John, was a prosperous glover who four years later became town Bailiff, but after this he gradually appears to have got into financial difficulties and it was left to William to restore the family fortunes from his success in the theatre. William was probably educated at Stratford Grammar School, acquiring what the playwright Ben Jonson described as Shakespeare's 'small Latin'; it was, however, enough to enable him to read the poet Ovid and the dramatists Terence, Plautus and Seneca in the original. There is at least one reliable report that Shakespeare worked as a schoolmaster for a time and we can be certain of his marriage, in 1582, to Anne Hathaway from neighbouring Shottery, and of the birth of their children, Susanna (baptised 26 May 1583) and the twins Judith and Hamnet (baptised 2 February 1585).

At some stage, probably following the birth of his children, Shakespeare decided to become an actor; we do not know precisely why or when, but there are records that between December 1586 and December 1587 five companies of actors visited Stratford and he may well have been recruited by one of them.

By 1592 Shakespeare had made his mark in London with three successful history plays: the First, Second and Third parts of *Henry VI* and he soon became a shareholder in a company of actors known as the Chamberlain's Men who established themselves at the Theatre, a playhouse owned by James Burbage in the northern suburbs of London. From his lodgings in Bishopsgate Shakespeare was able to work with the leading actors of his day including Will Kempe, a brilliant 'clown' and Richard Burbage, a fine tragedian, and many of the roles in his plays were, no doubt, written to suit their particular talents.

In the late sixteenth and early seventeenth century performing and creative artists were held in rather low esteem and in order to gain recognition relied heavily on support from noble patrons or from the Court itself; Shakespeare was no exception. In 1595 he was among members of the Chamberlain's Men who received a fee for two performances at Court; his play *The Comedy of Errors* was chosen for revival by the lawyers of Gray's Inn and it is highly probable that *A Midsummer Night's Dream* was commissioned in 1596 for the celebrations at the wedding of the daughter of Sir George Carey, patron of the Chamberlain's Men. Similarly, *The Merry Wives of Windsor* was probably performed at the Garter Feast in 1597 when Sir George was made a Knight of the Order.

The years 1593 and 1594 brought particular problems to the Chamberlain's Men because the plague forced the closure of the theatre for substantial periods. However, the enterprising Shakespeare showed remarkable adaptability and found a new patron in the youthful Earl of Southampton for whom he wrote and published two narrative poems, *Venus and Adonis* (1593) and *The Rape of Lucrece* (1594), and we think that Southampton enabled *Love's Labour's Lost* to have private first performances. It was in the difficult years between 1594 and 1599 that Shakespeare also completed *The Merchant of Venice, Romeo and Juliet, As You Like It, Much Ado About Nothing, Richard II,* the two parts of *Henry IV, Henry V* and, probably, *Twelfth Night.*

This remarkable achievement was only surpassed by Shakespeare's response to a new set of circumstances. In 1599 the Theatre was dismantled and its timbers ferried across the Thames to build the Globe on Bankside. Shakespeare was a 'householder' or part landlord and against a background of growing political tension the Chamberlain's Men were bribed to revive *Richard II* with its deposition scene as a comment on the Earl of Essex's political ambitions which led him to return to England against the Queen's wishes and to his rebellion and execution in 1601. Southampton, Shakespeare's patron and one of the supporters of Essex, was imprisoned and though the actors were not punished they had come perilously near to the power struggle.

When Elizabeth died in 1603 the Chamberlain's Men became the King's Men with the status of minor Court officials. *Macbeth* (1606) does honour to King James's union of the English and Scottish crowns, and the other great tragedies – *Othello, King Lear* and *Hamlet* – and the political Roman plays – *Julius Caesar, Coriolanus* and *Antony and Cleopatra* – all belong to Shakespeare's years at the Globe, together with what are sometimes called the 'problem' plays – *Troilus and Cressida, All's Well That Ends Well* and *Measure for Measure*. We know few details of Shakespeare's personal life during this period except that he was already making substantial investments in Stratford as a preparation for his retirement from London. The King's Men purchased a new *indoor* theatre, the Blackfriars, in 1608, and Shakespeare's final phase as a playwright seems to reflect the changed theatrical conditions for which he was writing. *Pericles, Cymbeline, The Winter's Tale* and *The Tempest* all benefit from production in a more intimate theatre space although it is not certain that these plays were exclusively written for the Blackfriars; the Globe continued in use until it was destroyed by fire.

That final group of plays, sometimes referred to as 'romances', have certain similarities and unifying features: they each concern royal children separated from, then reunited with, their parents and while the plays' plots are potentially tragic, their resolution is happy. Their subject matter is somewhat remote and improbable and there are strong supernatural elements; mysterious powers are at work of which the sea is often a major symbol, but the outcome invariably has a note of optimism and a hope for the future in the hands of the young generation. The romances also reflect changing tastes in theatrical entertainment.

Because *The Tempest* is the last complete play which we know Shakespeare to have written there has been a good deal of speculation as to its autobiographical nature. Prospero's famous speech in Act IV.i. 146–58 is often thought to be Shakespeare's 'farewell to the stage': a play concerning a magician who finally renounces his art and which has an unmistakably valedictory tone can reasonably be assumed to be the work of a dramatist at the end of his career. Nevertheless, it is dangerous to press this element of the play too far and critics are by no means agreed as to whether Shakespeare or Prospero is taking leave of his art and whether this is done with a sense of satisfaction, disillusionment, bitterness or mellowness. You will find helpful comments on these matters in the introduction to the recommended edition of the play.

By 1612, though he continued to visit London, Shakespeare seems to have had no residence there and apart from collaborating with John Fletcher on *Henry VIII* (1613) and *The Two Noble Kinsmen* (probably also 1613) he wrote no further plays. He died in Stratford in 1616 and left a will which still exists.

Though our sketchy knowledge of Shakespeare's life is tantalising, the essential fact to grasp in studying his plays is that he was basically a working play*wright*, a maker of plays, who responded to the pressure, changing tastes and conditions of the theatre of his day and it is to the nature of that theatre that we turn our attention in the Appendix.

2 THE BACKGROUND TO
THE PLAY

2.1 THE PLAY

The Tempest is perhaps the most literally wonderful of all Shakespeare's plays: an endless source of mystery and fascination to audiences, performers, scholars, poets, philosophers and a whole range of other creative artists. It is the supreme example of a new kind of seventeenth-century drama, the 'pastoral tragi-comedy', which Shakespeare perfected, a play which is more than simply a blend of tragic and comic elements but a work of art with quite distinctive qualities of its own. Our attention as an audience is constantly held by the rich *variety* of experience which the play offers, yet at no time do the contrasts seem inappropriate or clumsy. As with a great deal of popular entertainment, *The Tempest* involves both the natural and the supernatural worlds; its characters struggle not only against forces which they *can* control but against others which control them.

The enigmatic and dominating central character Prospero, has been eagerly undertaken by many great actors but equally carefully avoided by others. Recognised as one of the most demanding roles in English drama, the part of Prospero has been particularly associated with Sir John Gielgud in the latter half of this century and it is well worth listening to recordings of his interpretation of some of the play's speeches. *The Tempest*, however, is full of memorable characters, some very evil and others very appealing; there is rarely a scene in which we are not made to feel great sympathy for or antagonism towards the characters or to sense the tension that exists between them.

There are a number of other respects in which *The Tempest* is particularly effective theatrically: it contains exciting physical action, very amusing comic routines and marvellous language. All these are good reasons why your study and exploration of the play should, if possible, include some practical work and visits to productions. Much of the action depends on stagecraft and effects; I can well recall the thrill of seeing the opening scene for the first time in the theatre and the hilarity of some of the comic scenes when I saw the play produced by a French-speaking company with their rich and far better-preserved tradition of clowning. For most readers and theatre-goers, however, the greatest magic is contained in the *words* of the play: Shakespeare seems to have developed his powers to their ultimate.

It is hardly surprising that this many-faceted play with its elegance, earthiness, slapstick and deep seriousness should have attracted adapters in the worlds of ballet, opera and film, inspired composers to write new settings for its songs and provided a starting-point for such poets as W. H. Auden for new works of their own. The various modes of performance within a single play also make a constant challenge to directors and performers to create an entirely satisfactory production and the fact that they seem often to fail only makes the challenge stronger.

The world in which Shakespeare was writing and which he portrays to some extent in *The Tempest* was remarkably like our own. Great scientific advances had given man a vision of frightening powers; exploration had brought news of strange lands and stranger inhabitants – as fanciful as many of our science-fiction stories. Yet all this involved fierce debate as to the use and abuse of power, the nature of civilisation, the role of magic and the purpose of Art as opposed to Nature. These are some of the important issues discussed in *The Tempest* and although the greatest dramatists rarely provide *solutions* they do set out the *problems* in a vital way. It is true that *we* may not share the superstitions or the precise belief in the supernatural of Shakespeare's original audience but we cannot avoid the serious concerns with which we are confronted in *The Tempest*.

One of the play's most appealing strands is the love story concerning two of the young main characters, Ferdinand and Miranda. Both are the children of loving parents who desire the best for them. The love of the young couple is instant and passionate but Miranda's father urges restraint and is suspicious of his daughter's suitor. The tensions arising from so familiar a situation produce a human drama of perennial interest which Shakespeare handles with great skill and sensitivity; the playwright blends it with so many other dramatic ideas that his play is as vivid today as when it was first written.

There is a certain fascination for Shakespearean scholars in the fact that *The Tempest* was Shakespeare's last complete play, but unless you have a very extensive knowledge of all his plays it is unlikely that this line of approach will either appeal to or have much value for you. You must allow the play to make its impact on you and only make such deductions about it as can be reasonably sustained from the evidence of the text. It is difficult, however, to avoid coming to the conclusion that *The Tempest* is a most remarkable conclusion to an equally remarkable career.

2.2 ORIGINS AND SOURCES

When we come to study the text of *The Tempest* we can be confident that
modern editions are an accurate version of what Shakespeare actually
wrote and that the stage directions are what the playwright intended. This
is not always the case with Shakespeare but *The Tempest* was the first
play to be printed in the earliest edition of his plays known as the 'First
Folio'. This edition, compiled by two fellow-actors, Heminge and Condell,
appeared in 1623 and great care appears to have been taken in the preparation of *The Tempest*, including unusually meticulous punctuation and
stage directions. There is some speculation that the printed version of this
particular play was not based on a working copy used in the theatre, as
many of the other plays appear to be, but on a version which Shakespeare
was able to compile in the leisure of retirement. Whether or not this is
true we can be grateful that any edition of *The Tempest* which closely
follows the First Folio provides a particularly vivid insight into the playwright's theatrical imagination and how he wanted the play performed.

The first record we have of a performance of *The Tempest* is for
1 November 1611 before James I at Whitehall. This performance by
Shakespeare's company, the King's Men, may not have been the first but
other evidence shows that the play must have been written that year. The
Banqueting Hall at Whitehall would have created similar staging conditions
to those at the indoor Blackfriars Theatre and further experiments in
relatively elaborate scenic devices may well have taken place at *The
Tempest*'s next recorded performance, again at Court, in the winter of
1612-13. This was part of the celebrations of the marriage of James I's
daughter Elizabeth to the German prince, the Elector Palatine, and has led
some scholars to believe that the 'masque' section of the play was specially
added by Shakespeare for this event. It is far more likely, however, that
The Tempest which has a good deal to say about marriage, was simply felt
to be a particularly appropriate play for the celebrations and any evidence
that there was an earlier version of the play is extremely flimsy. You will
find an exhaustive discussion of this matter in Frank Kermode's introduction to the Arden Edition of the play.

Students are often puzzled as to the value of examining Shakespeare's
sources. There is obviously a certain fascination in seeing how the playwright has shaped sometimes dull and unpromising material into a successful
play as this can give insights into his craftsmanship. Sometimes, however,
Shakespeare used sources which were familiar to some of his audience and
in order to understand the impact of the play on that audience we also
need to be familiar with the ideas and attitudes embodied in those sources.
This is particularly true of *The Tempest* for although the play as we now

have it is one of marvellous complexity and originality there are four
obvious sources on which Shakespeare drew.

(a) Contemporary pamphlets

Shakespeare's imagination must have been gripped by accounts of some
extraordinary events which befell a fleet of nine ships sailing for the
colony of Virginia in 1609. In Silvester Jourdain's *Discovery of the
Barmudas*, the Council of Virginia's *True Declaration of the State of the
Colonie in Virginia* and a letter from his acquaintance William Strachey
Shakespeare would have read how on 25 July the flagship *Sea Adventure*,
carrying the admiral, Sir John Somers, and the new governor for the
colony, Sir Thomas Gates, had been separated from the rest of the fleet
in a terrible storm off the Bermudas (an area still associated with mysterious
events) and was feared lost. As the crew of *Sea Adventure* battled with
the storm for four days 'their clamours drowned in the winds, and the
winds in thunder' and flames appeared in the sky (St Elmo's fire); fearing
they were about to drown, the mariners drank to each other. Miraculously,
however, they managed to run the ship aground on an island, repair the
damage, save the cargo and continue their voyage to be reunited with the
rest of the fleet. Strachey's letter was eventually published as a pamphlet
whose title clearly shows the feeling that some Divine Providence had
shaped these events: *A True Reportory of the Wracke and Redemption of
Sir Thomas Gates*. The islands, always reputed to be so dangerous, had
proved a paradise to the mariners and their sense of wonder at their preser-
vation is easy to imagine.

Shakespeare, who had close associations with the Virginia company must
have discussed and mulled over these happenings and their implications
for he used them as the initial framework of his play. We shall note also
in the text where he has clearly taken a passage from one of the pamphlets
as his inspiration.

(b) Montaigne

Not only did Shakespeare make use of documented recent historical events,
he also made reference to topical issues. In William Strachey's letter there
was a passage in which the writer suggested that reforming and civilising
savage Indians was impossible. This question had been fully debated in an
essay by the French writer Michel de Montaigne (1533-92) entitled *Of
the Cannibals* which Shakespeare had clearly read in the English translation
of 1603. Montaigne described a society of American Indians, untouched
by Western civilisation but having a natural nobility which he regarded
as superior to the artificial values of the 'civilised world'. Shakespeare
directly transmits Montaigne's view of a Utopia through the speech of
Gonzalo, the 'honest old Councillor' in Act II.ii. 149-69 but the idea of

the 'noble savage' and of the conflict between Nature and Nurture or Art is never far from the surface. Caliban, the character in *The Tempest* described by Shakespeare as a 'savage and deformed slave' seems to swing between Strachey's and Montaigne's views: he has a kind of nobility but he is incapable of responding to the civilising influence of Prospero and Miranda.

(c) Ovid

Shakespeare was obviously familiar with the Roman poet Ovid's *Metamorphoses* both in the original and in Arthur Golding's translation, for he used sections of it in *A Midsummer Night's Dream* and *The Tempest*. At the climax of the play in Act V, scene i. (33-57) Prospero sets aside his magical art in a great speech which is clearly derived from a passage in Ovid. It is sublime verse in Shakespeare's version and his audience would have seen nothing unusual in the reworking of existing material in this way, indeed for some it would have added to the pleasure!

(d) The commedia dell'arte

As a member of a theatre company Shakespeare would have been particularly aware of the various performance styles and traditions which had influenced the profession. From about the 1550s a popular form of theatre that had its origin in Italy had made use of improvised acting techniques based on stock characters and simple plot outlines. In Shakespeare's day this was known as *commedia a soggetto* although since the eighteenth century it has been called *commedia dell'arte*. One popular short scene (*scenario*) *Li Tre Satiri* tells of an islander who plotted with two Europeans to steal a magician's book and control his spirits. They are eventually outwitted and the magician takes control. This story is rather similar to the main sub-plot of *The Tempest* and, perhaps even more significant, that sub-plot involving the 'clowns' Trinculo and Stephano demands very much the style of acting of the *commedia* with knock-about humour and improvisation.

2.3 THE TEMPEST AND RENAISSANCE IDEAS

Prospero, the central character of *The Tempest*, is sometimes represented as typifying 'Renaissance Man': that product of the rediscovery of classical learning and the subsequent burst of artistic and scientific creativity which influenced Europe in the fifteenth and sixteenth centuries. The Renaissance manifested itself in various ways in different countries: England's prime achievements were perhaps in music, literature, drama and science; new attitudes and widening horizons were gradually giving Man a differing image of himself and this is reflected in *The Tempest* in a number of issues.

(a) Science and Magic

In their attempt to investigate and explain the natural world, Renaissance scientists thought nothing of dabbling in the supernatural and occult. Science and magic were seen as complementary rather than contradictory and thus Prospero uses supernatural means to control natural forces. Shakespeare had probably heard of Dr John Dee who had died in disgrace in 1608. In his lifetime Dr Dee had owned a substantial library of science, philosophy and magic and had given invaluable help to early navigators through his understanding of geography and mathematics. Shakespeare's magician, Prospero, had also derived his power from books and had learned how he could influence world events as if he were a god. This essentially humanistic view of Man's powers was typical of a growing feeling of confidence as the frontiers of knowledge were advanced.

(b) Neo-Platonism and the Unities

Much of the impetus for Renaissance thinking came from efforts to assimi- late the ideas of ancient Greek philosophers into current beliefs. The teachings of Plato (427–347 BC) were consciously 'Christianised' and this 'neo-Platonism' (neo = new) involved methods of investigating natural phenomena. Another ancient Greek to influence sixteenth- and seventeenth- century views of drama particularly was Aristotle (384–322 BC) who had suggested a number of principles for the construction of plays in his *Poetics*. The neo-classical Unities of Time, Place and Action drawn from Aristotle were mostly ignored by Shakespeare but, as we shall see, he employed them with great effect in *The Tempest* demonstrating to his cultivated audience that he was perfectly capable of using such features to his advantage.

(c) Discovery, colonisation and travellers' tales

With advances in navigation and ever-increasing daring on the part of mariners, the known geographical world of Shakespeare and his con- temporaries was rapidly expanding. The discovery of areas of the 'New World' and of its inhabitants hitherto untouched by European culture gave rise to a number of moral and philosophical questions which the playwright examines in *The Tempest*: what right had explorers to colonise lands, exploit their resources and subjugate their native peoples? By introducing European culture to 'savages', were the early settlers liberating them or enslaving them? Was it possible for instance, that, in the new colony of Virginia, named after the Virgin Queen Elizabeth, a new Golden Age – the mythological age of innocence and plenty – could be established?

As we have seen, news of dangerous voyages, of strange discoveries and exotic places was spread by pamphlets and letters but there was also a strong tradition of oral travellers' tales. In the telling, such reports became distorted or exaggerated and in several of Shakespeare's plays there are references to extraordinary races of people: Othello speaks of 'men whose heads do grow beneath their shoulders' and Caliban in *The Tempest* is sufficiently grotesque to be mistaken for a half-fish. Caliban, however, is the original inhabitant of the island and his attitude towards other settlers and their attitude to him form one of the main tensions of the play.

3 SUMMARIES AND CRITICAL COMMENTARY

3.1 THE PLOT

The Tempest is one of the most Italian of Shakespeare's plays: the characters all have Italian names and have roles within Italian politics. There is no precise historical period indicated but Shakespeare makes at least one reference to contemporary England. The action of the play, apart from the first scene which is on board ship, is located on an island in the Mediterranean. Because of its position on the route from Italy to North Africa and its paradise-like qualities there is a legend that Shakespeare had in mind the Greek island of Corfu and Lawrence Durrell entitled his book about that island, *Prospero's Cell*. However, much of the detail of Shakespeare's island is clearly taken from his reading about Bermuda.

The play observes the three Unities: the action is confined to parts of the same location, the events actually occupy the three hours or so which the play takes to perform (unlike some of the other romances which have huge spans of location and time) and there is a single main plot to which all the subsidiary 'plots' belong organically.

Somewhat unusually the play *begins* with the catastrophe and much of the 'action' which has brought it about takes place *before* the play opens and is explained in a single long scene. Throughout the plot Shakespeare makes use of interesting parallels, especially between Caliban and Miranda and in levels of usurpation. The complex relationships will be better understood if we now examine the characters of the play – the *dramatis personae* – in the groups in which they appear:

1. *Mariners*

Ship-master	commander of the royal ships caught in a storm
Boatswain	whose job it is to give orders to the crew
Other mariners	an unspecified number of sailors

2. *Ship's Passengers* – Members of the Royal Court

Alonso	King of Naples, (he helped Anthonio to supplant Prospero)

Ferdinand	his son
Sebastian	Alonso's brother
Anthonio	usurping Duke of Milan, brother of Prospero
Gonzalo	an honest old Councillor who helped Prospero when he was supplanted by Anthonio – long-winded but worthy
Adrian Francisco	courtiers
Trinculo	the court jester (also on the ship, though
Stephano	the royal butler, usually drunk we do not see them)

3. *The Inhabitants of the Island*

Prospero	the rightful Duke of Milan (Milan is pronounced with accent on the *first* syllable) a magician who can control the elements
Miranda	his daughter who has been on the island since she was a young child and has only seen two 'men', Prospero and Caliban, in that time
Caliban	a savage who was the original inhabitant of the island and is now slave to Prospero. He is the son of the witch Sycorax who was banished to the island
Ariel	a spirit who can fly and change shape. Ariel was originally Sycorax's servant but as a punishment for disobeying her she had confined him inside a pine tree. Prospero rescued him and Ariel is now his servant

4. *The Spirits appearing in the Masque*

Iris	Goddess of the rainbow and Juno's messenger
Ceres	Goddess of crops
Juno	Queen of Heaven
Reapers and nymphs	dancers in the entertainment

A glance at this list of characters will already reveal some of the sources of dramatic tension in the plot. You should understand these as a basis for your study of the play. They are summarised below:

The Mariners

1. They are initially preoccupied with the dangers of the storm and cannot attend to the complaints of the passengers. The importance of their royal passengers creates an extra strain on them;
2. Later in the play they are still filled with wonder at their miraculous escape.

Passengers and court

3. Terrified but helpless in the storm – they get in the way of the crew;

4. Thankful to be alive once they land on the island but as they are now in small groups they are *uncertain who has survived*;
5. Varying degrees of *guilt* concerning Prospero, whom they believe to be dead;
6. Gonzalo's awareness of the guilt of others in Prospero's overthrow;
7. Gonzalo's tendency to talk a great deal in a tense situation.

The Islanders
8. Caliban and Ariel are both servants and may wish to regain their freedom;
9. Caliban's resentment of other settlers on 'his' island;
10. Prospero's feelings towards the King and his brother for their part in his overthrow;
11. Miranda's ignorance of the world in general and her limited experience of men in particular;
12. Prospero's protective feeling towards Miranda, his only daughter. He is a widower and in human terms Miranda is 'all he has left';
13. Prospero's potential for revenge now that he has developed strong magical powers.

During the course of the play these tensions sustain the interest of the audience and gradually move towards a resolution. Other tensions emerge as the plot develops and frequently the characters are in great danger. In order to examine the play in more detail we shall first look at the plot in outline.

3.2 PLOT SUMMARY

Before the play begins
Prospero, the Duke of Milan, had tended to neglect his public duties in order to study his valuable collection of occult books. His brother, Anthonio, had plotted with Alonso, the King of Naples, to take over the dukedom and because Prospero was still loved by his people they dared not simply kill him. Prospero had been forcibly taken on board a ship with his infant daughter Miranda at midnight, then set adrift with the child in an open boat with no sail. Secretly, however, a loyal courtier, Gonzalo, had put some fresh food and water, some rich clothes and a selection of Prospero's most treasured books in the boat. Father and daughter are washed ashore on an island where Prospero has developed his magic powers, released Ariel from bondage and attempted to educate Caliban. Caliban has learned language but has responded to Prospero's kindness by attempting to rape Miranda so Prospero has made him his slave.

During the course of the play

Twelve years after Prospero's banishment the Court of Naples is returning by sea from Tunis where Alonso's daughter, Claribel, has married the King. Prospero, with Ariel's help, raises a great storm which drives the ship onto his island and Alonso (together with Sebastian, Anthonio, Gonzalo and other courtiers) is brought ashore at one part of the island, Ferdinand at another point and Trinculo and Stephano at yet another point. The mariners stay safely with the ship but the rest of the fleet continues its voyage presuming the royal ship lost.

Miranda is horrified by the storm and the suffering it has caused but Prospero explains to her the events of the past twelve years and engineers a meeting between his daughter and Alonso's son, Ferdinand. The young couple fall instantly in love though Ferdinand is still grieving for the supposed loss of his father. Prospero puts obstacles in the way of the growing relationship in order to test Ferdinand's sincerity and strength.

Alonso and the rest of his court are the next characters on whom Prospero works through Ariel. The King is dejected by the loss of his son and Gonzalo talks at length about the nature of the island and the miracle of their safety. Overcome by Prospero's charm the entire court falls into sleep – with the exception of the evil Anthonio and Sebastian. Anthonio now incites Sebastian to kill Alonso and take the crown for himself but the plot is foiled by Ariel at the last minute and in a later scene Ariel appears as a vision, accusing Alonso, Anthonio and Sebastian of their wrongs. In confusion they continue their search of the island.

Caliban, smarting under Prospero's discipline, has met Trinculo and Stephano who have introduced him to drink. Thinking Stephano a god, Caliban persuades them to join him in a plot to murder Prospero and take possession of the island. Their drunken clowning is interspersed by the tricks which the invisible Ariel plays on them but Prospero very nearly forgets the threat which they pose.

Prospero, having decided to dispose of his magic powers and return to a normal life allows Ferdinand and Miranda to be betrothed and has his spirits perform a beautiful masque in celebration. Prospero ends the show abruptly as he recalls the plot against his life and transforms the spirits into hunting hounds to torment the plotters. Prompted by Ariel's pleading, Prospero hastens to end the suffering of his other enemies and his old friend Gonzalo as he prepares to renounce his magic. Under Prospero's charm, the court is brought to the spot where Ferdinand and Miranda are playing chess together. Prospero thanks the faithful Gonzalo and confronts and forgives his enemies, demanding his dukedom back. Alonso breaks his pact with Anthonio and, seeking forgiveness of Prospero, is reunited with his son Ferdinand. Alonso and Prospero are united in happiness for their recently-betrothed children and Miranda is amazed at the beauty and nobility of mankind. The mariners arrive to tell their remarkable story.

The least desirable elements of mankind are unchanged by their experience: Anthonio and Sebastian remain silently unrepentant; Trinculo and Stephano are brought grovelling to the feet of their superiors. Caliban regrets his misplaced confidence and re-inherits the island while Ariel's final task before freedom is to provide a calm sea-passage back to Naples for the court.

Prospero is left alone to ask for our applause and prayers as the 'stage magic' we have witnessed comes to an end.

Important note

All the information contained in *both* parts of this summary is contained within the text itself. It is a particularly valuable exercise for you to study *how* and *when* Shakespeare provides this information.

Since the eighteenth century it has been usual for 'scenes' in printed plays to indicate a change of physical location but prior to that it was more usual for a fresh 'scene' to begin whenever a new character entered or a character left the stage. It is useful to think of plays as being comprised of such units as indicated by Professor Brooks in his Introduction.

3.3 SCENE SUMMARIES AND CRITICAL COMMENTARY

Act I, scene i

Summary

The stage represents a ship at sea in a terrible storm. Above the noise of the thunder and wind the Master gives his orders to the Boatswain who relays them to the mariners. Whistles are blown and the mariners work at the rigging. Anxiously, the King Alonso, Sebastian, Anthonio, Ferdinand, Gonzalo and other courtiers enter looking for the ship's Master but they simply impede the work of the crew and the Boatswain shouts at them to remain below. Gonzalo, who always has a great deal to say, takes comfort from the Boatswain and refers to a proverb which suggests he is more likely to hang than drown. As the activity increases the 'landlubbers' again become a nuisance and there is much cursing. The mariners declare that all is lost and whereas the Boatswain suggests comfort in a drink, everyone else goes to prayers. The ship is abandoned as the scene ends.

Commentary

It is particularly difficult to gain an impression of the impact of this exciting scene from a quiet reading. The shouted dialogue, the sound effects and the movement of the characters can produce a stunning atmosphere in performance and you must attempt to recreate this in your mind. The scene is one of striking naturalism: Shakespeare has taken most of the nautical detail and the technical terminology from a contemporary handbook of navigation and he provides a realistic picture of people behaving under great stress. Already a number of personal characteristics begin to emerge: Gonzalo's tendency to be long-winded, coupled with his gentleness and optimism; Anthonio and Sebastian's sheer unpleasantness. We learn little of the king or his son.

At the end of the scene we are left in suspense as to the fate of the ship or its passengers; the abruptness and violence of the beginning and end of the scene create a theatrical shock of great power. Shakespeare has clearly used information from the Bermuda pamphlets. Note how the mariners drink as they feel the ship sinking, and the confusion seems to demand a resolution in subsequent scenes. The scene is written in prose although lines 11–19 can be rearranged as verse.

Act I, scene ii

Summary
The location changes to the island and in Shakespeare's theatre a 'discovery place' may well have represented Prospero's cave or cell. As they enter Miranda is pleading with her father to calm the storm if he has caused it, because she has seen the ship driven ashore and all on board abandon her. Prospero reassures Miranda that all is well and goes on to tell her that the time has come to explain to her the reasons for their being on the island, the origins of his magical powers and the cause of the tempest. Miranda responds as her father gently questions her as to what she can remember from her distant past and she becomes enraptured as he explains how Alonso and Anthonio had robbed him of his dukedom. Sometimes almost incoherent with anger, Prospero continues his story and Miranda questions him. Exhausted by the effort of listening and by the struggle to come to terms with so much that is new and shocking, Miranda falls asleep just as Prospero is saying that he must grasp the opportunity that has brought his enemies to the island.

Prospero then summons Ariel who reports in great detail how he has carried out his master's orders with regard to the storm and ensured that the passengers are now distributed around the island. Prospero says that there is more urgent work to be done but Ariel complains and reminds Prospero that he has promised him freedom. This inopportune objection enrages Prospero who reminds Ariel very forcefully of the debt he owes him and threatens terrible punishment. Contrite, Ariel becomes compliant and is sent to change his shape to that of an invisible sea-nymph.

Miranda is now woken and goes with her father to visit their slave, Caliban. Caliban emerges from his den cursing and in response to Prospero's threats of punishment complains that Prospero and Miranda have taken possession of *his* island and that because of their initial kindness to him he had shown them all the natural resources of the island, only to be exploited and made their slave. Prospero retorts that this is his punishment for attempting to violate his daughter's honour and Miranda reminds him how she had patiently taught him language. Caliban, not to be outdone, replies that the only benefit of that is that he can now curse! Furiously, Prospero orders him to fetch fuel or endure torment.

Ariel enters, singing and playing, followed by the King's son Ferdinand, who is in a trance-like state, affected by the music which speaks of his 'dead' father. Miranda sees Ferdinand and is deeply attracted by his appearance and when he sees her he thinks her a goddess. Watched by Prospero who reveals to the audience that he wants them to fall in love, Ferdinand and Miranda talk wonderingly and shyly together. Ferdinand, thinking himself already king of Naples, promises to make Miranda his queen. Believing things to be moving too quickly Prospero interjects bad-temperedly and pretends to Miranda that she is foolish to fall in love with the first young man she has met. Overcoming Ferdinand's attempts to resist, Prospero makes him a prisoner, accusing him of a plot to usurp him and orders him into his cell. Miranda pleads with her father and comforts Ferdinand while Prospero, in 'asides' to the audience and Ariel, reveals that this is all an 'act' and that he is grateful to Ariel for having brought about this relationship.

Commentary

Shakespeare follows the shortest scene in the play with by far the longest scene, drawing the audience into the atmosphere and detail of Prospero's magical island by a remarkable change of pace and time-scale. Making enormous demands on the actors, the playwright achieves his exposition in a number of long speeches. The audience, like Miranda and Ariel, are forced to listen and follow. With the opening line of the scene we are introduced to the theme of Prospero's Art: magic, and the magician wears a special garment as a symbol. By the conclusion of the scene we have not only learned how Prospero has acquired his Art but how he can now apply it. We also see contrasting aspects of Prospero's character: his gentleness and love towards his daughter are evident. He lays aside his magic garment as he addresses her, he pays tribute to her behaviour and he becomes understandably edgy at that most difficult moment in a caring father's life when his daughter meets her future husband. But we also see Prospero's fury and strength in his treatment of both Ariel and Caliban – indeed he appears remarkably harsh. His rebuke to Ariel may seem unreasonable but such is the power of evil in this play that it can only be overcome with firm resolution. Prospero has learned from experience that human kindness is not enough and it is vitally important to his purpose that he exploits the opportunity that has now arisen to work on his enemies.

By the conclusion of this scene we have met all the play's main characters, apart from Trinculo and Stephano, and have insights into the complex relationships and tensions between them. As Prospero gives an account of what has happened he finds it impossible not to become emotionally involved. He begins calmly, plying Miranda with questions rather like a psychiatrist, but when he starts to recall Anthonio his grammar and syntax become confused: the sentence which begins 'my brother and thy uncle' (66) is never completed and he is side-tracked into a series of parentheses. He continues with a string of metaphors, anacolutha (broken sentences) and images of ever-increasing urgency and excitement which become difficult to follow and require Miranda's prompting questions to bring him back to the point. It is small wonder that Miranda is exhausted by the combination of shocking revelation, concentration and emotional involvement with Prospero's predicament.

In contrast, Prospero's tirade to Ariel shows the powerful magician very much in control. This section is an ingenious device of Shakespeare's to give important background information but it also introduces the subject of Sycorax, the source of evil and black magic over whom Prospero has triumphed. Through Ariel, Prospero has all his former enemies in his power. By separating Alonso from Ferdinand he will make them psychologically vulnerable in their grief thus making contrition and reconciliation more possible. Ariel is sent away to become a Nymph of the sea but he is somewhat puzzlingly invisible to all but Prospero. Shakespeare thus establishes the convention that Ariel is now invisible to all other characters in the play.

A major theme of the scene is usurpation. Prospero recalls bitterly how his authority was usurped by Anthonio but Caliban recollects equally bitterly how his possession of the island was usurped by Prospero. Ironically, Prospero treats Ferdinand as a potential usurper. In Caliban's speech (331-45) we are also introduced to the problem of colonisation; Caliban describes Prospero's treatment of him as if he were a patronising colonialist exploiting all the natural resources of the island. Prospero's initial behaviour had been benevolent, he sought to impart *his* culture to the savage native. His attempt had been hopeless and all he had achieved was to give Caliban a language in which he could curse. There is clearly a contrast in the effect of the education which Caliban and Miranda have received but Miranda's cultural upbringing is not necessarily superior to the more natural learning of which Caliban is capable. *She* is not particu-

larly well-equipped to live in the real world of men and *he* is not without
sensitivity. Although Caliban is a creature of the earth and his concerns
exclusively involve the physical, his language is often astonishingly beautiful
in its earthiness and he shows great powers of observation.

The language of the entire scene demonstrates Shakespeare's verse at
its most flexible, powerful and subtle. He evokes a complete magic with
the alliteration of:

> Sit still, and hear the last of our sea-sorrow (170)

or the simple addition of 'crying' to the sentence:

> The ministers for the purpose hurried thence
> Me, and thy crying self. (131-2)

Great venom is contained in 'A rotten carcass of a butt' (146) and
Prospero's magnificent rebukes of Ariel and Caliban give vivid and colourful pictures of interactions with the natural elements:

> Thou dost; and think'st it much to tread the ooze
> Of the salt deep,
> To run upon the sharp wind of the north,
> To do me business in the veins o' th' earth
> When it is baked with frost. (252-6)

It is important for you to become attuned to the shifting textures and
robust strength of the language in your early readings of the play.

For revision purposes especially it is as well to recollect this long scene
in its units:

(a) *Prospero/Miranda*. Note how the powerful impact of the sea is carried
over from the first scene. Prospero's 'sea sorrow' has brought him to the
island where he has perfected his knowledge. Your recommended edition
of the play guides you through the complexities of Prospero's monologue
with helpful paraphrases – but if these are not available to you you should
attempt your own.

(b) *Prospero/Ariel* – there is a difference between Ariel, the pliant, airborne
spirit and Caliban, the unwilling slave. Notice Ariel's description of his
manipulation of the 'wreck' and its similarity to the travellers' tales we
have examined. It was Prospero's Art which liberated Ariel from Sycorax's
black magic but it is through Ariel that Prospero will achieve his ends.

(c) *Prospero/Caliban/Miranda* . Only after his attempted rape of Miranda did she view him as a 'villain . . . I do not love to look on' (310) and Prospero's attitude towards him changes. Caliban's hatred is equally intense and thus he always poses a threat. He acknowledges the power of Prospero's Art but never ceases his rebellion.

(d) *Ariel/Ferdinand*. This brief moment is important for here we see the first of the ship's passengers affected by the spell of the island. Significantly, Ariel sings a 'magic song' - a popular device in the seventeenth-century theatre invariably sung by a treble voice. Ferdinand is charmed and the words of the song speak of a 'sea change' which might apply to all the mortal characters in the play. We shall need to examine further the particular role of music in *The Tempest*.

(e) *Ferdinand/Miranda/Prospero*. One of Prospero's ultimate objectives is to reverse all the events of twelve years previously and to see his daughter married to the heir to the throne. He has brought them together by magic but this does not extend to *making* them fall in love. As David Hirst puts it: 'But they do fall in love, Miranda for the first time, Ferdinand in a far deeper way than he has experienced before. Prospero breathes a sigh of relief. His aside, "It works", is charged with significance.' Prospero tests their love, forcing the young couple to learn more of their mutual affection and dependence. Initially Ferdinand sees Miranda as a goddess - part of the island's enchantment and he is always aware that his 'spirits, as in a dream, are all bound up' (491) but Miranda is already moving away from her father's world towards her 'brave new world'.

Act II, scene i

Summary

The stage now represents another part of the island and we see the royal party, of whom we had a brief glimpse in the storm. Ferdinand is missing, presumed drowned. Accordingly, his father Alonso is in a state of deep depression. Gonzalo attempts to comfort the king by drawing attention to their miraculous escape in which even their clothes are unharmed but he is constantly mocked by witty and unkind interjections and asides from Sebastian and Anthonio. Alonso can bear all this talk no longer but Francisco describes how he saw Ferdinand swimming strongly. Alonso refuses to believe that Ferdinand may have survived and Sebastian adds to his misery by saying that he only has himself to blame for insisting on marrying his daughter to an African, thus necessitating a sea voyage.

Gonzalo rebukes Sebastian for his insensitivity and then speculates on how, if he had control of the island, he would create a new Golden Age of innocence. At this point Ariel enters, invisible to the actors, and with magic music induces sleep in all but Anthonio and Sebastian who offer to stand guard. While the king is asleep Anthonio subtly persuades Sebastian that he should kill the king, his brother, and take the throne for himself. Inspired by Anthonio's example in having supplanted *his* brother Prospero, Sebastian is on the point of carrying out the assassination when he hesitates. In that moment Ariel, seeing the danger, sings in Gonzalo's ear and wakens him, and he in turn wakes Alonso. Caught with their swords drawn, Sebastian and Anthonio make an absurd excuse that they heard a frightening noise. Alonso orders a continuation of the search for his son while Ariel goes to report to Prospero what he has seen and done.

Commentary

This is a notoriously difficult scene both for students and performers; you should not be unduly worried if at first reading it seems largely unintelligible! Much of the difficulty is caused by the constant play upon words, especially in the form of puns, indulged in by Anthonio and Sebastian. Such witty and complex dialogue was typical of Elizabethan and Jacobean court circles. Where words are obscure to us or have changed their meaning the whole drift of a conversation may be lost; in such situations we have no alternative but to tease out the meaning by reference to notes in a good edition of the play. In performing it is surprising how much can be understood at first hearing but in rehearsal actors will often improvise the scene in their own words to establish the best intonations and phrasing. This is a good idea for students to follow and it will help to establish which lines are said quietly between Anthonio and Sebastian, who are clearly standing some distance apart from the others, and which lines are interjected into the conversation of the other characters. You will find it particularly interesting to play the part of Gonzalo and to explore ways in which to make the pauses in his speeches credible. You may well come to the conclusion that the pace of his lines is more hesitant and ponderous because of his age.

The scene falls into two major sections: Gonzalo's attempts to comfort Alonso, and their consequences (1-191) and the plot against Alonso (192-end). Alonso is the focus of the action in both sections although he says very little. At first the emphasis is on his profound sense of loss and this theme is taken up again in the final lines of the scene. In the previous scene we have heard of what Prospero had lost and now as he begins to work on Alonso to bring him to a state of realisation and contrition it is necessary for the king to experience misery and suffering. The predicament in which the other characters find themselves and the mood of their king prompts Gonzalo, Francisco, Anthonio and Sebastian to reveal more of their true personalities. Gonzalo and Francisco are positive, if sometimes clumsy, in their attempt to find good and hope in the situation whereas Anthonio and Sebastian seem negative in every aspect of their behaviour. Their malice and sneering are in stark contrast to Gonzalo's integrity and by their attitude to Alonso it is difficult to remember that Anthonio had been a joint conspirator with the king in the overthrow of Prospero. Shakespeare's original audience would have noticed the way in which Anthonio, a duke, demeans himself by permitting Sebastian, his inferior, great familiarity and it is significant that both are immune to the gentle spell of Ariel's music which induces sleep.

In the first part of the scene, four speeches stand out from the tiresome verbal gymnastics of the courtiers. Gonzalo's opening lines (1-9) are somewhat wordy, well-meaning and over-stated so we can well understand Alonso's weary reply 'Prithee, peace'. By the time that the king explodes in a graphic mixed metaphor:

> You cram these words into mine ears against
> The stomach of my sense. (109-10)

he has extended the image of Sebastian's earlier remark:

> He receives comfort like cold porridge (10)

The remainder of Alonso's speech (109-16) is a very moving revelation of his sense of loss. Francisco's description of Ferdinand's possible survival (116-25) has both the formality of a symbolic picture, which in Elizabethan and Jacobean art was called an *emblem*, and a blend of realism and idealism. The emblematic quality of the speech is fitting as an address to a king but also as an image of hope. Gonzalo's speech (149-69) which he has attempted to start a few lines earlier and contains some sarcastic interruptions, is typical of the man's fertile imagination.

This speech is based on a passage in Montaigne's *Of the Cannibals* which we have discussed in 2.2 (b) but also draws on the legendary idea of a Golden Age of innocence. The idea that man in his primitive state, uncomplicated by education, culture, trade or politics - could live in a state of blissful harmony was attractive to early settlers discovering native inhabitants untouched by European civilisation. In Prospero's account of his usurpation and our subsequent view of Anthonio and Sebastian we see how corrupt European society can be; but on the other hand we have seen that the native Caliban is far from a state of innocence. There is always this tension between the potential beauty of the island and the evil it contains and whereas it seems paradise-like to Gonzalo, it is treacherous for Alonso.

With the entry of Ariel and the magic charm represented by the music, the mood of the scene takes on an altogether more sombre note. This

change is reinforced by Sebastian's unexpectedly gentle and solemn
speech:

> Please you, Sir,
> Do not omit the heavy offer of it.
> It seldom visits sorrow; when it doth,
> It is a comforter.   (194-7)

Here Sebastian, unwittingly perhaps, hints at the healing process which
lies behind Prospero's scheme. In dramatic terms, however, this now
presents an ideal opportunity for a plot. As the great poet and critic
Samuel Taylor Coleridge (1772-1834) pointed out, the ensuing moments
in which Anthonio works on Sebastian, tempting him with the idea of
the crown, are very similar to the scene in which Lady Macbeth manipulates Macbeth. Notice how the precise nature of Anthonio's suggestion
slowly dawns on Sebastian who extends the idea of sleep to symbolise
his gradual realisation of the truth. Anthonio, in this most theatrical of
plays, uses the image of investiture in other men's robes to make usurpation seem attractive. Sebastian admits to the sloth (224) which, as he
had been born a king's brother, inhibits ambition; so Anthonio's main
aim is to awaken this ambition both by reasoned argument (for example,
lines 245-61) and enticement (for example, lines 273-6).

Prospero, through Ariel, must now frustrate their merciless plans and
the incantation-like lines which awake Gonzalo (301-6) produce a moment
of tension and excitement in contrast to the dark murmurings of the plot.
The spluttered excuses of Sebastian and Anthonio are as shifty as they are
themselves. Anthonio realises that lions are a more credible explanation
than bulls and Sebastian clutches at this more plausible straw. Gonzalo,
however, may have heard humming, as though he were attuned to the
natural, healing music of the island. The final pace of the scene is very
vigorous and Ariel's rhyming couplet gives momentum to the characters'
exits.

Act II, scene ii

Summary
We now have to imagine the stage to be yet another part of the island.
Caliban, who has been ordered by Prospero to gather wood, is seen carrying
his load and uttering curses against his master. He describes how he is
controlled by Prospero's spirits and, thinking he sees one approaching,
falls flat on the ground. The new character is, in fact, Trinculo the king's
jester looking for shelter from another storm. He stumbles across Caliban
and ruminates as to what sort of creature he is. A thunderclap sends

Trinculo crawling under Caliban's gaberdine (cloak) for shelter. A third character now enters: this is Stephano, the king's butler, singing drunkenly. Attracted by Caliban's groans Stephano investigates the huddled figures and in his intoxicated state is baffled by the four legs and two voices he perceives. Trinculo recognises the voice of Stephano and there is a comic reunion in which they imagine that they and a cask of wine are the only survivors.

Caliban, having been made to drink from Stephano's bottle, thinks that he has found a god who can be his master and rid him of Prospero. He kneels to Stephano who assures him that he has come from the moon. In awe, Caliban promises to serve Stephano and enable him to exploit all the resources of the island. While Trinculo laughs at the absurd situation Stephano enjoys Caliban's worship and leads him on to make promises of allegiance. The scene ends with the exit of Caliban drunkenly celebrating his freedom in song, followed by Trinculo and Stephano who believe they now rule the island.

Commentary

By the conclusion of this scene all the play's main characters have been introduced and the subsidiary, parallel plot has been established. Although the scene begins with Caliban's venom towards Prospero and the subsequent action results in a threat to Prospero's power the predominant tone is richly comic. Students would be well advised to try out the scene in performance to experience the knockabout humour and vulgarity of the stage 'business' and language at first hand. Some of the humour derives from the contrasting characters: Caliban, strangely poetic and gullible; Trinculo, with his quickfire wit, his topical jokes (28-35) and quick movements; Stephano pompous, slow and self-confident as drunkards often are. The audience, however, also laughs with Trinculo as, under the influence of drink, Caliban worships the worthless Stephano.

The audience is prepared for the arrival of Stephano with his bottle by Trinculo's simile of the large black cloud which looks like an old wine skin on the point of bursting. Thereafter the predominant power in the scene is drink, the supreme substitute for thought and wisdom, but the thunder-cloud itself is a reminder of Prospero's power which has been so graphically outlined in Caliban's first speech (1-14).

In certain respects the entire scene is an ironic comment on the arrogant conduct of colonists and the naivety of the natives. Thus it is also a parallel to what had occurred between Prospero and Caliban. 'Indians', (that is, either Red Indians or men from the West Indies) had been an object of fascination in England since 1576 where they were exhibited for profit. Trinculo refers to this (30) and Stephano equates Caliban with an Indian (59) making it quite clear that Caliban is not fish-like in appearance (although he may smell like one) but the Indian 'savage' of the travellers' tales. Colonists were often received with kindness, and they themselves acted kindly initially. In both cases this was often followed with treachery. Caliban indicates that he is willing to do what, twelve years earlier, he had done for Prospero (150-74) and this speech looks back to the speech in Act I (I.ii. 333-9) in which Caliban tells of his sharing the island's plenty with Prospero. Caliban is primitive and his view of the world is that there are frightening, evil spirits and there are gods. Once he is sure that Trinculo and Stephano are *not* the spirits he thought them to be (14 and 119) he can worship them as gods. But, as Stephano reminds us (68), Caliban has acquired language so that in spite of his deference to the two clowns he can manipulate *them* for his own ends by his powers of persuasion.

Stephano's attitude by which he virtually proclaims himself king is high-handed and condescending. He exploits Caliban's primitive religion for his own ends and enjoys his moments of petty power. Trinculo already sees the potential tragedy of faith in such a person:

> A most ridiculous monster, to make a wonder of a
> poor drunkard. (188)

and it is a long time later and after much suffering that Caliban comes to that realisation.

Stephano's belief that he is now King introduces again the recurrent theme of usurpation and this develops powerfully as the collusion between Caliban and the clowns grows into a plot to overthrow Prospero. You should also note the extensive use of prose dialogue by Trinculo and Stephano in contrast to the verse of Caliban.

Act III, scene i

Summary
The action takes place outside Prospero's cell. Ferdinand enters carrying one of many heavy logs which Prospero has ordered him to pile up, on pain of punishment. As he works Ferdinand, in a soliloquy, says that his thoughts of Miranda make his painful task a pleasure. Miranda enters and is upset to see Ferdinand's task. Telling him that Prospero is safely studying his books, Miranda urges him to stop and talk with her; but unseen to them, Prospero has entered to overhear their conversation. The growing love between the two young people becomes obvious as Miranda offers to help carry logs and Ferdinand forbids it, saying that her presence dispels fatigue. Ferdinand asks Miranda her name and she, disobeying her father, tells him. Ferdinand responds by declaring how he admires her

more than any woman he has met and Miranda says that although she has never met another man except her father, she cannot imagine a better than Ferdinand. Tenderly they now express their deep love for each other and the watching Prospero reveals his pleasure in 'asides' to the audience. With promises of devotion Miranda and Ferdinand agree to become betrothed and then leave the stage in different directions. Prospero is delighted but says that he has more to achieve before supper-time, so returns to his books.

Commentary

This is, perhaps, the finest love scene which Shakespeare ever wrote and it is almost as if he, in the character of Prospero, is admiring his own artistry as he watches this

> Fair encounter
> Of two most rare affections. (74-75)

The scene begins with one of several curious parallels in the play: Ferdinand, like Caliban in the opening of the previous scene soliloquises as his enforced slavery for Prospero takes the form of carrying logs. But his reaction is entirely different: Caliban, as he has informed us earlier, uses language to curse. Language in Ferdinand's usage is a graceful medium for the expression of love. Through a series of antitheses (1-9) he speaks in courtly language, idealising his love and sharing his thoughts with the audience. Scholars have debated furiously the precise meaning of the lines

> But these sweet thoughts do even refresh my labours,
> Most busiest, when I do it. (14-15)

but the reading suggested by the *Arden* edition and the editors of the *Macmillan Shakespeare* seems the most convincing in the context of the scene to follow 'I forget' (13) which is clearly a disguised stage direction meaning that Ferdinand has allowed himself to stop working. *Now* he says that his 'sweet thoughts' are actually *more* active when he is busy.

The 'fair encounter' between Ferdinand and Miranda extends the use of courtly and formally patterned language. Miranda's suggestion that the logs which Ferdinand has carried will 'weep for having wearied' him as they burn is a *conceit*, a fanciful image with which courtly literature abounded. Ferdinand's beautiful declaration of love (38-48) begins with a clever pun on Miranda's name and emphasises its points with gentle alliteration. 'Concealed couplets' also occur in the scene (for example 24-5) giving it a formality appropriate to courtly love. You should look for other examples of this subtle use of rhyme.

The emotional impact of the scene on Prospero and the audience is all the greater for its restraint and what gives it particular poignancy is the meeting between the innocence of Miranda (48-57) and the experience of Ferdinand (39-46). True love surmounts both to create a spiritual union and Prospero's comment takes the form of a benediction, like that used at Divine Services:

> Heavens rain grace
> On that which breeds between 'em (75-6)

Another parallel with the actual marriage service occurs when Ferdinand calls upon all the witnesses he can to hear his profession of love (68); this is extended in the promises they make to each other and the *visual* image of Prospero officiating.

The earliest stage directions we have for the scene simply stipulate Prospero 'at a distance, unseen', but later editors, like those in the *Macmillan Shakespeare* have suggested that Prospero appears 'above', possibly on the small balcony at the rear of the stage. This entirely reasonable conjecture certainly adds to the scene's impact and Prospero's reaction to the behaviour of his daughter is of great significance. As is so often the case in love, parental wishes and instructions are forgotten (37 and 58) but Miranda's love for her father is undiminished. This is surprising in the light of Prospero's initially aggressive attitude towards Ferdinand but parental ties are very strong. In his joy at his daughter's evident happiness, Prospero mellows, and even overlooks Miranda's disobedience. Her tears (76) tell us of her tensions.

At the opening and the end of the scene we are reminded of one of the play's great paradoxes. Prospero has acquired his magical powers from his books and he must return to them constantly. Yet in doing so he once lost his dukedom. Had he been at study he would not have witnessed this scene and it is important for him to engage with the real world again to see the achievement of his ends. The urgency which he feels is summed up in the final line of the scene.

Act III, scene ii

Summary
From this point in the play onwards the action moves backwards and forwards between the various groups of characters in the different parts of the island until they are brought together in the final scene.

In this scene the focus is on Caliban, Stephano and Trinculo who enter the stage which here represents an unspecified location on the island. Both Stephano and Trinculo have been drinking and are very merry while

Caliban, who is unused to alcohol, has drunk himself almost speechless. Stephano encourages Caliban to drink more and promises him a post as his officer. Trinculo mocks this absurd idea and Caliban, asking to lick Stephano's shoe in a gesture of obedience, reveals his dislike for Trinculo. The tension between Caliban and Trinculo grows and Stephano, taking Caliban's side, warns Trinculo to be careful what he says.

Caliban then begins to tell Stephano more about his slavery to Prospero, a subject which they have obviously discussed before; and tries to persuade Stephano to murder Prospero. However, Ariel has now entered, invisible, and interjects with audible comments like 'thou liest'. This enrages Caliban and Stephano who mistakenly think the remarks come from Trinculo and it eventually comes to blows. Caliban, with Trinculo forced to stand well away, is finally able to tell Stephano that he must kill Prospero during his afternoon sleep, destroy his books and take his beautiful daughter for himself.

Stephano agrees to do so and they begin to sing. Stephano is reconciled with Trinculo and they are entranced by Ariel's music. Caliban explains how the island is often full of sweet sounds and they follow the music, intent on the destruction of Prospero.

Commentary

This is a scene of great contrasts: at one level highly comic and yet deadly serious; earthy and prosaic at times and at others richly poetic. The entry of Stephano, Trinculo and Caliban shows them at their most absurd, the contrast between the behaviour of the hardened drinkers and the inexperienced drinker is comic and as the scene progresses it has the ingredients of a 'slapstick' farce. Caliban's adulation of Stephano and his contempt for Trinculo produce a tension between the three characters from which much of the comedy derives and there is an absurd gap between what Caliban *thinks* Stephano is capable of doing and the *reality* of the situation. Stephano, for example, is most unlikely to bite Trinculo to death (34)! Caliban's constant reference to Stephano as 'thy Greatness' emphasises his subservience and shows his determination to serve Prospero no longer.

Again, Caliban shows that his reaction to new settlers is to share with them the secrets of the island (69) but to continue to maintain that it is *his* island (54-5). As he calms down his anger turns to evil cunning, and the speech (88-105) in which he gives details of Prospero's movements, books and daughter sets up resonances from the second scene of the play. Prospero's power and its dependence on books, his gift of language to Caliban and the parallel situation between Caliban and Miranda in relation to Prospero are all beautifully illustrated here.

The reconciliation between Trinculo and Stephano is represented in the harmony of singing but the crude music they use is sharply contrasted with the magic music of Ariel. Caliban emerges as a far more sensitive and imaginative being than the pathetically cowering Stephano or Trinculo and his great speech (137–45) is one of the most wonderful moments in the play. This evocation of the effect of music shows that Caliban is capable of rich imagination; that he is not all earth-bound and that he does indeed have elements of the 'noble savage'. Stephano's response is not only trite, he reveals that he really inhabits a world of fantasy and the *real* plot is already becoming a delusion. Caliban, however, ensures that the scene ends on an ominous note and Ariel now has another usurpation attempt to thwart. In extreme situations men jostle for power and this scene is a comic reminder of the malice of Anthonio and Sebastian.

Act III, scene iii

Summary
Alonso and his court enter the stage which *may* represent the same part of the island as in the previous scene. Exhausted by their fruitless search, they rest. Quietly, Anthonio and Sebastian continue to plot. At Prospero's command Ariel causes a banquet with various spirits to appear and Prospero watches unseen as the banquet vanishes just as Alonso and the others are about to feast. Ariel now addresses Anthonio, Sebastian and Alonso, accusing them of their crimes and telling them that he has made them mad as a punishment. Only virtuous lives and repentance in the future can save them. Anthonio and Sebastian rush out to fight what they imagine to be demons while the despairing Alonso determines to drown himself and lie beside Ferdinand whom he believes to be drowned. Gonzalo, not hearing Ariel's words, attributes all this behaviour to the guilt of his fellows.

Commentary
In terms of stage action this scene seems very static on the page but it is a very important point in the spiritual journey of Alonso and in Shakespeare's theatre it demanded elaborate scenic effects. The predominant idea is sin and its consequences. Alonso and his court have been in a 'maze' (2), a madness brought on by Prospero's Art which has ensured that their search has been in vain. For all except Gonzalo, this loss of direction is representative of moral chaos. Now fading hope has led to physical weariness and despair. Alonso's opening speech (4–10) demonstrates his spiritual desolation. They are tempted by a representation of worldly pleasures, and they fall – just as Adam and Eve fell from grace

with the eating of an apple while by contrast Christ rejected the temptation of food in the wilderness – so we see the sinners attracted to take food from the illusory banquet. In the state of depression which ensues, Prospero can convict Alonso, Sebastian and Anthonio of their sin thereby offering an opportunity for contrition, repentance and redemption.

This allegorical interpretation based on Christian theology (with which the average member of Shakespeare's audience would have been far more familiar than a modern audience) is suggested by key words: 'worse than devils' (36), sin (53), perdition, that is, damnation (77), trespass (99), guilt (104); although the precise nature of the Divine power is kept vague by the use of such terms as Destiny (53), Fate (61) and The Powers (73). In one sense the scene, in which we see several men who have followed their own wills now in Prospero's power, is a microcosm of sinful Man in the hands of God.

Prospero works on Alonso and the others as he has on Caliban and Ferdinand. In Act I, scene ii (489) Ferdinand has explained how his 'spirits, as in a dream, are all bound up' and the same sensation accounts for the confusion of the King and his court; Ariel says he has made them 'mad' (57). This mental confusion is partly brought about by magic music. The 'Marvellous sweet music' (19) to which Gonzalo refers has been prepared for by Caliban's memorable speech in the previous scene. The 'harmony' (18) accompanies the appearance of 'a living drollery' (21) – an animated puppet-show which is a supreme example of illusion. It is both a mockery and an invitation to the banquet which in itself is unreal. At this point in the scene the 'real' and 'imaginary' worlds become confused. There are constant reminders of the fantastic tales of such islands brought back by travellers and of fabulous beasts. Rather like science-fiction, the frontiers of exploration have sometimes overtaken and sometimes lagged behind the imaginary. Gonzalo, for instance, now seems ready to accept that there are, indeed men 'Whose heads stood in their breasts' (47) and such is the effect of Prospero's island and its spells that minds are prepared to believe almost *anything*.

The response of the various characters is crucial to an understanding of the scene. Gonzalo hears the music and sees the banquet but does not hear Ariel's accusation. He cannot understand Alonso's distraction (94) and yet recognises symptoms of guilt.

Anthonio and Sebastian seem devoid of compassion and are incurably malicious. They remain defiant and unabashed, beyond the reach of redemption, and they acquire a frenzied courage:

> I have made you mad,
> And even with such-like valour men hang and drown
> Their proper selves. (58–60)

Alonso continues the references to music as he describes the thunder as a 'deep and dreadful organ pipe' which 'did bass my trespass' (99). This means that he now feels his great sin as being the foundation of everything in his life just as a deep note on an organ provides the harmonic foundation of a melody. His contrition, the result of Prospero's 'high charms' (88) has brought him to a state where he can receive forgiveness and where through his *loss* he can now *find*.

It is worth noting that the scene envisages a number of non-speaking parts and that there is a single line (40) assigned to Francisco. Without these parts, Gonzalo's final lines (106-8) would be nonsensical but it is a fascinating question for you to consider why Shakespeare persists with these silent characters.

Act IV, scene i

Summary

In front of his dwelling-place, Prospero is now revealing to Ferdinand and Miranda his approval of their betrothal. In giving his daughter to Ferdinand he warns the young man to respect her chastity until the wedding ceremony is over and Ferdinand vows to do so. Prospero now sends Ariel to fetch Caliban with his conspirators and then summons spirits to perform a masque for the entertainment of the lovers. The masque takes the form of a celebration of marriage and fertility and the lovers are transfixed by it. Prospero, however, suddenly recalls the plot against his life and orders the masque to end. He answers Ferdinand and Miranda's concern for his mental state in a speech which dwells on the ephemeral nature of theatre and life and they leave him. Ariel enters and describes how he has led Caliban, Stephano and Trinculo through all kinds of discomfort before leaving them in a stagnant swamp. Delighted, Prospero now orders Ariel to hang gorgeous clothes on a line by his cell. Predictably, and to the fury of Caliban, Stephano and Trinculo are distracted by this 'trash' before Prospero's spirits in the shape of hunting hounds, chase them, howling, from the stage.

Commentary

In this scene the major strands of the play are approaching their climax: the love of Ferdinand and Miranda is no longer frustrated by Prospero although he makes it perfectly clear that they must await marriage for its final consummation (14-22); Prospero's control of his enemies is nearly complete and the threat against his life reaches a crucial stage.

The opening of the scene assumes some conversation that has taken place off-stage, so the audience is left to imagine the initial reaction of the lovers to Prospero's apparent change of attitude. This is relatively unimportant compared with the central idea of the sanctity of marriage and its prerequisite – the essential, pure state of pre-marital chastity. It seems highly probable that *The Tempest* was first performed at a betrothal celebration (2.2) and the scene captures that sense of anxiety for propriety typical of the anxious father. After Prospero's initial lecture to Ferdinand he still cannot resist another stern warning (50–4) when he obviously sees the embraces becoming a little too passionate. The idea of self-control is reinforced by Ferdinand's reply.

As we have seen, it has been suggested that the 'masque' section of the scene was added at a later date and is therefore something of an excrescence in the play. The masque certainly does present some problems for a modern reader or audience both on the page and in performance but its inclusion in the play seems perfectly consistent with Shakespeare's and Prospero's designs. Music and theatrical effects are two of the most potent agents of Prospero's Art and it is inconceivable that he would allow the betrothal of his daughter to pass without bestowing on the young couple 'Some vanity' of his Art (40-1). Furthermore, ever since 1605, a new vogue for spectacle in the form of masques involving dance, music and visual display, had emerged in England. Court masques had existed for some time but the playwright Ben Jonson (1572-1637) and the stage designer Inigo Jones (1573-1652) had revitalised the Stuart masque so that the elaboration of a central symbolic and mythical 'device' in visual terms had become a powerful art form, standing for vital issues in the power politics of the time. Shakespeare's move to an indoor theatre together with changing tastes opened up the potential of such entertainment and as a practical man of the theatre he was unlikely to let such new developments pass him by.

The difficulty for the modern student is to reconstruct imaginatively what a masque performance looked and sounded like. At this point it is sufficient to note that it was a colourful and elaborate spectacle making use of such effects as moving clouds, characters descending from 'heaven', a great deal of music (much of the dialogue may well have been sung or spoken over music) and dancing (see 5.4). If this act of imagination seems pointless or tiresome to you, imagine trying to convey the best features of your favourite record and associated 'video' by asking someone simply to read the words of the song on the record sleeve!

The masque is an act of celebration in a pastoral and allegorical mode. Using rich images drawn from Nature Shakespeare elaborates upon the two blessed states of marriage and fertility. The plot of the play, moving swiftly to the dénouement, is suspended for a while by the leisurely pace of the masque. It is, of course, an illusion – but for a while it seems like Paradise to Ferdinand (124) and this makes its crumbling all the more significant. In one sense the masque is a 'masque within a masque' because the entire play has masque-like elements but the masque which Prospero presents to the young couple shows him particularly in his role of stage-manager, totally in control. However, as in other aspects of his life, Prospero is only partially successful. The unreal illusion which he creates causes him to forget the real attempt on his life just as his earlier retreat into a world of books made him neglect his real political role and cost him his dukedom. The anguish and disturbance shown by Prospero as he suddenly recollects Caliban's plot is a very important moment in the play. On the surface it seems like over-reaction but his realisation that he has risked losing his life and his daughter must revive painful memories and remind him that his magic has failed him.

Disenchantment with Art and a sense of the ephemeral nature of theatre and life prompt Prospero's wonderful speech (146-58), so often considered as Shakespeare's own farewell to the theatre. You should note the clear references to the elaborate scenic settings of masques (151-3) and the way in which the entire theatrical process becomes a metaphor for life. This metaphor has recurred throughout Shakespeare's work and it climaxes here in a memorable statement concerning illusion and impermanence. In the final lines of his speech (158 onwards) Prospero shows a great weariness, as though all his creativity has left him drained but he then needs to be alone with his spirit Ariel in order to concentrate all his attention on the final stage of his project. Ferdinand and Miranda's farewell is a formal expression of their unity.

The entry of Caliban and his rabble is skilfully prepared by Ariel's description of his tricks (171-84) yet Prospero's short venomous soliloquy about Caliban before his entrance is of great significance. Caliban's nature (188) has not responded to Prospero's nurture (189). With Miranda it was different, she has grown wiser and more beautiful under Prospero's care and education but Prospero's Art has failed to transform Caliban. He has remained not so much in a state of primal innocence (the state in which theologians believed Adam to be before his 'Fall') as in a state of sin. The complex issues raised by this speech have resonances throughout the play. One such echo is of Prospero's comment in Act III, scene iii, (35-6) when he suggested that Anthonio and Sebastian are 'worse than devils'. Shakespeare does not intend us to think that Caliban is necessarily worse than a cultivated, 'civilised' man, on the contrary, we have seen that Caliban has elements of the 'noble savage' whereas with far less excuse for devilish conduct, Anthonio and Sebastian are devoid of nobility.

Shakespeare's audiences were accustomed to a theatrical tradition in which evil figures were also comic. The ensuing incident with its obscenity, witty patter, comic routines and topical jokes is, at one level, pure clowning. However, for Caliban it is a moment of revelation in which he realises what idiots he has taken as gods. His carefully calculated plot is ruined by the vanity and stupidity of Stephano and Trinculo who make a comic comment on their role as potential usurpers by attempting to dress up in 'borrowed robes' (an image Shakespeare uses in *Macbeth*). Some of the impact of this scene is very difficult to recreate in performance today because of the obscure meanings of some of the lines but the incident should provide a brief moment of fun before the serious intentions of Prospero are resumed.

Act V, scene i

Summary

Prospero re-enters the same setting, wearing his magic garments. Ariel informs him of the condition of the King and his followers, urging Prospero to feel sympathy for them in their predicament. Prospero says that he intends to forgive them and dispatches Ariel to bring them to him. In a long soliloquy Prospero speaks of his control over Nature and of his intention to renounce magic now that his 'project' is completed.

Ariel brings the King and his company to stand, charmed, before Prospero and after kind words to Gonzalo Prospero accuses and then forgives Alonso, Sebastian and Anthonio. Ariel then dresses Prospero in his robes as Duke of Milan and goes to fetch the Master and Boatswain of the ship. As the consciousness of Alonso and his courtiers returns Prospero reveals himself to them. Alonso begs forgiveness, restoring Prospero's dukedom, Anthonio and Sebastian are sullenly unrepentant while Gonzalo is too moved to speak.

Alonso tells Prospero of the loss of Ferdinand, and Prospero keeps him in suspense by saying that *he* has lost a daughter. He then pulls back a curtain to reveal Ferdinand and Miranda playing chess together. In a touching reunion, Alonso asks forgiveness of Ferdinand and is introduced to Miranda who is fascinated by the sight of so many mortals.

The Boatswain then enters and explains that the ship has miraculously escaped damage. Alonso is still incredulous when Ariel drives in Caliban, Stephano and Trinculo. All three are contrite, Caliban realising his stupidity. Prospero invites the court to spend the night in his cell where he will relate the events of the past years before their departure for home where he will regain his position and prepare for death. Ariel is to provide calm seas for the voyage and then be free. Caliban will regain the island.

In an epilogue to the audience Prospero invites our prayers and applause.

Commentary

In an important renaissance essay entitled *A Compendium of Tragi-comic Poetry* (1601) Giambattista Guarini set down certain principles for the writing of tragi-comedy, a new kind of drama of which *The Tempest* is an example. As we conclude our Act-by-Act consideration of the play we can see how Shakespeare used Guarini's neo-classical model and adapted it to his own purposes. The first Act was to contrast tragic and comic material, thus preparing the audience for the mixed genre; the second Act must introduce new material which is still relevant to the main plot; the third Act should contain comic plotting with the kind of intrigue familiar in comedy; the fourth Act should show the greatest threat, with tragedy narrowly averted and the fifth and final Act should be concerned with a happy outcome involving an unexpected twist concerning the well-being of the virtuous characters and the conviction and repentance of the guilty. You should note that in the context of this formula the word 'comic' implies having the ultimate result of a happy outcome rather than 'funny'.

Having averted the greatest threat to his life at the conclusion of the previous Act, Prospero prepares for the dénouement – the final resolution of the plot. The fifth Act consists of a single scene of six units plus an epilogue: 1 – 32; 33 – 57; 58 – 171; 172 – 215; 216 – 55; 256 – 319, each unit introducing a fresh combination of characters. The opening shows Prospero as the renaissance *mage* – scientist, philosopher, white-magician – speaking of his 'project' as if it were an experiment in alchemy (the pseudo-science which sought to create gold). He wears his magic robes to emphasise the role he is playing and to give greater significance to his later change of clothes. Much of the interpretation of the play by a student, actor or director depends on an understanding of the precise nature of Prospero's 'project'. At one level his motives are political: he seeks to retrieve his dukedom and establish Miranda in the royal house of Naples; on a wider front he seeks to confront his enemies and bring them to repentance. In the process, however, Prospero has had to establish control over both Nature and his inner self. He seeks to restore harmony, and that can only be achieved through forgiveness. Ariel prompts his sympathy for the suffering his enemies have undergone (17-19) and Prospero unexpectedly reveals that 'The sole drift of my [his] purpose' (29) goes no further than ensuring *penitence* in his enemies. He chooses 'virtue' rather than 'vengeance' as the way forward.

Prospero's 'Farewell to his Art' (33-57) is, as we have seen (2.2(c)) Shakespeare's reworking of Medea's speech in Golding's translation of *Metamorphoses* which begins 'Ye Ayres and Windes: Ye Elves of Hilles, of Brookes, of Woods alone'. For our generation, obsessed by ideas of 'originality' and surrounded by dire warnings of the consequences of plagiarism, this seems strange. But in Shakespeare's time joint authorships and borrowing from other authors were common and for the more sophisticated members of the audience the recognition of the neo-classical source was something to be savoured.

In performance, this speech, with its seventeen majestic lines before a definite stop (50), is one of the supreme moments in the English theatre and if you are unable to experience this for yourself you should at least take the time to read it aloud several times. The invocation of all the powers of Nature spoken by the single actor alone on stage produces an atmosphere of spine-tingling magic as it gathers momentum. The demands of phrasing and breath control for the actor are tremendous and at the conclusion of the speech Prospero seems utterly drained.

The significance of this speech for the whole play is far greater than a passing theatrical experience however – for Prospero has already acknowledged how transitory the theatre is (IV. i. 148-58) – this is a major turning-point and an unexpected one. Prospero invokes all the powers and spirits over which, by diligent study, he has gained control. He refers to this as 'my so potent Art' (50) but the next moment it is 'this rough magic' (50). It has served its purpose in finally bringing his enemies under control yet twice already in his lifetime he has nearly lost everything by studying his books instead of involving himself in reality, so now the book which Caliban recognised as the source of Prospero's power (III.ii. 91 and 94) is finally to be cast aside. Here Prospero uses an echo of the lines in which Alonso last left the stage (III.iii. 101), a note of irony which reinforces the image of finality. Prospero can only achieve so much by his white magic and he now intends to manipulate his enemies' senses once more before returning to what the human mind and soul must achieve unaided.

At the entrance of Alonso and the court Prospero initiates the redemptive process by invoking the healing power of music. He must express his love and gratitude to Gonzalo first: and in so doing he continues the shedding of tears by which Ariel was so moved (15 and 16) and which promised a more conciliatory end to the play. However, when he turns on Alonso, Anthonio and Sebastian he can scarcely contain himself; Prospero's self-control, a quality which he has had to learn and has constantly urged on Ferdinand, is put to the test as, for the second time, he confronts his enemies with their sin (cf. III.iii. 53-60). No insult could have been sharper than his description of Anthonio as 'unnatural' (79) – a loaded word which implied a denial of everything good; but the most remarkable thing is that this label is coupled with words of forgiveness.

Ritually Prospero now leaves his role of magician and resumes his role of duke by his change of costume. Meanwhile Ariel's song of freedom prepares us for the almost total silence with which he disappears at the end of the play. As Gonzalo returns to consciousness his words seem to echo the sense of being in a maze which he expressed at the opening of Act III, scene iii. He feels a moral confusion from which only a 'heavenly power' can lead him.

Moral order is restored in Alonso's plea for forgiveness but Sebastian still fails to recognise the power of good and thinks that 'The Devil speaks in him' (129). This is what draws from Prospero a sharp 'No' (129).

Prospero has led Anthonio and Sebastian to a point where they can find grace and forgiveness but, like leading a horse to water you cannot make it drink, so he cannot force them to find redemption.

The scene is impregnated with the Christian idea of losing in order to find. Shakespeare and his audience would have been familiar with the famous parables of Jesus on the subject and His saying:

> For whosoever will save his life shall lose it: but whosoever will lose his life for my sake, the same shall save it. (Luke IX, 24)

The words 'loss', 'lose' and 'lost' appear frequently between lines 135 and 152, stressing the totality of Alonso's deprivation. Only *now* can he begin to *find* himself and his son. Similarly, Prospero had to lose his dukedom and his daughter in order to discover the truth about his life and his values, and to establish a new order.

It is heavy dramatic irony with which Prospero tells Alonso of the loss of Miranda and a strong visual image is created by the brief glimpse of the lovers at play before they are aware of the onlookers. Miranda's reaction to the assembled company (181-4) strikes a new note of optimism and hope. Even Anthonio and Sebastian are part of her 'brave new world' and we feel that this point of entry into that world is really the culmination of Prospero's project. It is for the new generation to make something of their world now that for Prospero's generation 'every third thought' will be their grave (312).

The speed with which Ferdinand and Miranda have moved from love at first sight to betrothal is overlooked in the general rejoicing, which is reinforced by Prospero's insistence that the past must be forgotten (see 197-9). The final assurance that harmony has been restored comes when Gonzalo eventually finds his tongue (200)!

When the Master and Boatswain enter we learn the extent of Prospero's control of the elements. As he promised Miranda in Act I, ii. 'There's no harm done' (I.ii. 15) and the Boatswain's description accords with the facts recorded in one of Shakespeare's main sources (see 2.2. (a)). The miraculous survival of the ship is only one of the many achievements of Ariel; his quiet interjections (for example 240) remind Prospero and the audience of the debt owed to him. Note also how Alonso repeats the image of the maze in line 242.

The final resolution of the plot reintroduces Caliban who will reinherit the island. Caliban's first comment (261) concludes the parallel between himself and Miranda which began with the contrasting accounts of their education, continued in the accounts of their first meeting with men and ends with the similarity between Caliban's 'these be brave spirits' and Miranda's 'brave new world'. Nurture has achieved little for Caliban's nature and this is emphasised by the striking similarity between the remarks of Anthonio and Sebastian (263-5) and those of Trinculo when he first stumbled upon Caliban in Act II, scene ii, 18-42. However, Caliban is sufficiently changed by the experiences of the play to recognise his gullibility and his need for pardon. In using the word grace (296) he suggests that divine forgiveness leading to a new life is implicit in his intentions.

Ariel's final charge and silent disappearance into the air seem almost like ingratitude. Ariel's slavery has been the price for his delivery from Sycorax, whose black magical power Prospero still vividly recollects (see 268-71) and the emotionless exit of Ariel is in keeping with his nature. The play ends with a calm and quietness in direct contrast to its opening.

Epilogue

The final twenty lines spoken directly to the audience by the actor playing Prospero can be interpreted as the conclusion of an autobiographical play by Shakespeare in which, before returning to retirement in Stratford, he apologises to James I, an acknowledged expert in demonology, for trifling with magic. Such an interpretation rarely rises above mere speculation, whereas it is perfectly possible to treat these lines as those of an actor renouncing his stage magic. What he, in essence, is saying is

> Here I stand, removed from the story I've just unfolded. Just as I gave up my powers in the story so I now appear stripped of the illusion. You could say that my achievement as an actor is like the successful outcome of the plot of the play. I behaved well in my imaginary part and hope that I acted it well. In the *story* my reward was to return to Milan and to complete the parallel *you*, the audience need to release me from the imprisonment of failure as an actor. In the same way that Ariel ensures a calm voyage and brings my project to a happy end you must ensure the success of my theatrical presentation by your applause. I am now stripped of the stage-magic which might have obtained such applause by evil means and I must endure the sense of despair which I shall feel if this prayer to you fails – nevertheless I can still, like every man, appeal for Christian mercy and I appeal to you for such mercy, just as you would wish for mercy to obtain forgiveness for your trespasses against others.

(NB You may well have to re-read this attempt to paraphrase Prospero's speech several times). You may recognise an allusion to the Lord's Prayer, which includes the phrase 'forgive us our trespasses as we forgive those who trespass against us,' suggesting that one of the levels of interpretation of the play is as a Christian allegory. However, this Epilogue is as enigmatic as the rest of the play and this is, perhaps, the secret of its richness.

4 THEMES AND ISSUES

4.1 DISCORD, HARMONY AND RECONCILIATION

The Tempest opens with total confusion: action, sounds and the elements produce a sense of discord in the universe. This theme is picked up by Prospero in Act I, scene ii, when his account of the treachery of his brother frequently breaks down in confused syntax and lines of thought; it is reiterated by Ariel in his description of the storm (I.ii. 196-206). For the first half of the play Prospero seems at odds with everyone except Miranda and Gonzalo and even his relationship with his daughter becomes strained while Gonzalo wanders in a maze. Discord and moral chaos predominate; bitterness, hatred and suspicion are always close to the surface. The island seems hostile.

At the entry of Ferdinand in Act I (376) there is already a suggestion of the possibility of harmony. Only a few lines earlier Prospero has been threatening Caliban with torments which will provoke a 'din' but now there is gentle music, indicating that the island might be a benign place. Healing sleep induced by music overcomes Alonso and Gonzalo in Act II, scene ii, but Anthonio and Sebastian create further discord as they seem to be immune to Prospero's charm. The same charm works on the courtiers in the final scene of Act III, convincing them of their sin, yet although the music has been full of harmony, the desperate exit of Anthonio and Sebastian strikes a discordant note.

From the opening of Act IV Prospero begins the work of reconciliation; first with Ferdinand, who is already in perfect concord with Miranda. His plan is interrupted by the memory of Caliban's plot, so there is a return to anger and revenge before the important speech of Ariel at the beginning of Act V re-establishes the mood of forgiveness. Prospero's compassion is prompted by Ariel's reaction to the predicament of the courtiers and is extended to his former enemies in his speech (V. i 58-83) introduced by music. By the conclusion of the play order has been restored and there is the promise of calm seas as opposed to the tempest with which the play opens. Anthonio, Sebastian, Trinculo and Stephano remain fundamentally unchanged by their experience but this does not diminish the power of the ending. It is far more significant that Prospero has reached a point in his life when he can *offer* forgiveness and hence the possibility of recon-ciliation. The final harmony comes from the reuniting of distanced families and, for the central figures, the substitution of love for hate.

4.2 MAGIC
(NB You should re-read 2.3(a) before reading this section.)

Charms and spells were part of the everyday experience of Shakespeare's original audience. In the small towns, court records were full of accusations of witchcraft; the King himself had written a book on the topic. Frustrated lovers, disappointed farmers, the sick and those in pain frequently hoped that a charm or potion would solve a problem for which we might now turn to science for a solution. Magic assumed the existence of a spirit world which was far more widely accepted than nowadays. The boundaries of sorcery and science were very uncertain.

Two powerfully opposing forces use magic in *The Tempest*: Sycorax the witch and Prospero. Sycorax's charms are evil, black magic. They are composed of things considered loathsome or associated with darkness and night:

> As wicked dew as e'er my mother brushed
> With raven's feather from unwholesome fen . . . (I.ii. 322-3)

> All the charms
> Of Sycorax, toads, beetles, bats, light on you; (I.ii. 340-1)

Prospero accuses Caliban's mother of having committed the ultimate in witchcraft – intercourse with the devil:

> Thou poisonous slave, got by the devil himself
> Upon thy wicked dam, (I.ii. 320-1)

He persists in such insults to Caliban's evil parentage, reiterating them whenever they meet or the thought of Caliban crosses his mind. He refers to him as 'a freckled whelp, hag-born' (I.ii. 284), 'Hag-seed' (I.ii. 366), 'A devil, a born devil' (IV. i. 188), 'demi-devil – For he's a bastard one' (V. i. 272) and 'thing of darkness' (V. i. 274). All these suggestions play upon the idea that witchcraft and black magic involve trafficking with the Devil and that hell contains many devils who can be conjured up. In his description of the mariners in the storm Ariel tells how one man cried out

> 'Hell is empty,
> And all the devils are here'. (I.ii. 214-15)

and both Stephano (II.ii. 58 and 100) and Trinculo (II.ii. 90) are convinced that devils are plaguing them.

Through her devilish magic, Sycorax has acquired great power. A worshipper of the heathen Patagonian god Setebos, she

> could control the moon, make flows and ebbs,
> And deal in her command. (V. i. 270-1)

Shakespeare paints a very conventional picture of this witch: foul, old and bent-backed, capable of 'mischiefs manifold and sorceries terrible' (I.ii. 265) and, for a character who does not actually appear in the play, he takes great care to emphasise the evil magic of which she was capable, so that her influence is strongly felt. Consorting with the Devil was widely held to be a means of acquiring knowledge and, predictably, Sebastian mistakes Prospero's profound understanding for such ill-won power when he says 'The Devil speaks in him' (V. i. 129). In certain respects Prospero's power *is* like that of Sycorax: Prospero uses it to torment his enemies just as Sycorax had punished Ariel (see I.ii. 270-82) and there is a nice parallel between their spells when Caliban refers to 'wicked dew' (I.ii. 322) and Ariel recalls fetching dew for Prospero from 'the still-vexed Bermoothes' at midnight (I.ii. 228-9).

Prospero, however, has acquired his magic, which he refers to as his Art, by diligent and methodical study. He explains this in his long discourse to Miranda in Act I, scene ii. It is a magic based on an understanding of natural laws of science and it is *more* potent than the black magic of Sycorax. Caliban says:

> I must obey; his Art is of such power
> It would control my dam's god Setebos,
> And make a vassal of him. (I. ii. 374-6)

In your study of the play you should note the occasions when Prospero speaks of his Art and what he says about it. We are introduced to the topic with the very first words which Miranda speaks to her father in the second scene of the play and there is a constant, strong *visual* reminder of that Art in Prospero's magic garment and magic staff. Prospero uses his magic in a number of ways: he makes himself invisible, he disarms his enemies, he charms men's minds. Predominantly, Prospero uses magic to control the *natural elements* and the *spirit world*. According to his long speech in V. i. 34-50 and from his various conversations with Ariel we are led to understand that it is *through* his control of spirits that Prospero has controlled Nature. Ariel, who is a spirit, is Prospero's chief agent in causing the tempest from which the play takes its name and all the other manifestations of his 'so potent Art' depend on the 'aid' of 'elves', 'demi-puppets' and other spirits (see the speech just cited).

The most spectacular demonstrations of the Art are the storm itself, the frequent charm of music, the ability to watch his enemies (see II.i. 298-300) and the various theatrical devices. Prospero refers to the masque, which is entirely enacted by spirits, as 'some vanity' of his Art (IV. i. 41), the whole incident reminding us of the special kind of magic practised upon his audience by the playwright himself. Prospero also uses his spirits to plague and torment his enemies. Notice how many times Caliban mentions this and how he thinks Trinculo a spirit when he first sees him approaching.

The question remains why Prospero decides to renounce his Art; why, looking back on all he has achieved, he simply calls it 'rough magic' (V. i. 50). For the answer we must consider the nature of his 'project' which reaches a crucial point at the opening of Act V. Once the aims of the project have been achieved and once the *limitations* of the magic have been acknowledged, then the Art has no further use. You should examine, therefore, all that Prospero *does* achieve and all that he *fails* to do in your attempt to answer the question.

4.3   THE STRUGGLE FOR POWER

Prospero's enforced stay on the island and his subsequent project are the result of an act of political treachery by his brother and King. This act sets in motion a whole chain of events, each of which could involve further usurpations. Prospero is robbed of his dukedom and in turn displaces Caliban. Anthonio and Sebastian plot to supplant Alonso; Trinculo and Stephano plot to usurp Prospero's power. Prospero accuses Ferdinand:

> Thou dost here usurp
> The name thou ow'st not, and hast put thyself
> Upon this island as a spy, to win it
> From me, the lord on't. (I.ii. 456-9)

Prospero's sensitivity to threats stems from his painful memory of the unnatural behaviour of his brother but the whole play shows the lengths to which men will go to seize power. In Jacobean times this involved the upsetting of a divinely ordained sense of order which began with God and the angels and was mirrored on earth by a triangle with the monarch at the apex. To remove a man from his rightful place in this scheme of things was not only seen to be a serious crime but one which would reap punishment. Prospero aims to restore political order; and this means regaining his posittition *and* leaving the island to its rightful owner, Caliban. By engineering the meeting and hence the union of Miranda and Ferdinand, he is making the political future of his family much more secure.

From the issues we have considered so far it can be seen that *The Tempest* explores many aspects of the nature of power and the desire to obtain it. Prospero studies to control Nature but those who plan to seize power by 'supplanting' (note the occasions when this word is used) others are shown to be corrupt and unscrupulous. Prospero's description of Anthonio's tactics in Act I, scene ii. (79-87) is a particularly telling example of the portrayal of political intrigue.

4.4 LOVE AND MARRIAGE

In my introduction to this play (2.1) I suggested that some of its appeal derives from an effective love story and in 2.2 we saw that it had one of its first performances, if not its first, at a marriage celebration. The love affair between Miranda and Ferdinand passes through three phases: their initial *meeting* (I.ii.), their *testing* (III.i.) and their *reward* (IV). Prospero manipulates all three but it is made clear that he cannot *make* the young couple fall in love. Understandably Prospero is possessive and protective towards Miranda, especially in the light of Caliban's attempted rape. It is easy to overlook the fact that Shakespeare also provides a sympathetic portrait of the love between father and daughter in the very deep and tender relationship that Miranda and Prospero enjoy. This is also duplicated in the mutual love of Ferdinand and Alonso.

Ferdinand is expected to subdue the Caliban within him. His courting of Miranda is conventional – he praises her beauty in extravagant terms, his view of future happiness is expressed in hyperbole (a form of exaggeration):

> Might I but through my prison once a day
> Behold this maid. (I.ii. 493-4)

He describes how she has changed his perception of every experience (see III.i. 1-15), he expresses his love in witty conceits (see III.i. 33-4) and he humbly offers himself as her servant. Miranda responds with similar humility and you should study again the Commentary on Act III, scene i. to remind yourself of the refined and controlled passion of the two lovers.

Prospero's repeated insistence on pre-marital chastity almost seems unnecessary in the light of the mutual respect and gentility Ferdinand and Miranda have shown. Miranda is portrayed as all innocence but the courtly Ferdinand is unlikely to take advantage of her. It is precisely the self-discipline and appropriateness of behaviour that Shakespeare makes so attractive. Only by such elevation of *chastity* can *marriage* be celebrated as consummation.

Marriage follows solemn vows made by both lovers, although we do not witness the final ceremony. Prospero's masque reinforces all the attitudes towards love and marriage that have governed his conduct towards the young couple: in his warning to them (IV. i. 12-23) he has promised only discord and 'weeds' if they fail to comply with his demand for chastity – the masque offers the alternative of harmony and rich issue once the marriage rites are completed. Ferdinand and Miranda are the focus of the attention: the moment of their betrothal is sufficiently important to warrant the arrival of goddesses. The mythological figures present the themes – illicit love is to be avoided, the contract of marriage includes vows of pre-marital chastity, rich blessings of daily happiness and children will be the reward. During the course of the masque Ferdinand expresses harmony with his new father-in-law (IV. i. 123-4) and in a very moving moment of the final scene (V. i. 214-16) Miranda is accepted lovingly by Alonso.

4.5 NATURE, NURTURE, ART AND CIVILISATION

If man is to live in harmony with the rest of Nature he cannot allow it to run wild. He must cultivate the crops, tend the woodlands, control the rivers and so on. In short man must *nurture* Nature, shaping, caring and modifying. This does not mean that Nature on its own is often not very beautiful and fine but that what is 'natural' must sometimes be ordered so that it reaches its full potential.

Man himself is also, of course, a *part* of Nature and were *he* allowed to run wild, simply following his 'natural' inclinations, chaos would result. The purpose of civilisation is to bring order and to enable man to use his natural inclinations within a framework of control. Man *nurtures* his children so that they also achieve their full potential. This may take the form of parental care and education, such as Prospero gives Miranda, and the process of civilisation also involves the acquisition of the type of *self-*

control which Caliban has not achieved. Like the rest of Nature there is much that is 'naturally' good in every human but there is also a considerable tendency towards evil. Caliban personifies this; the wild man, capable of some sensitivity and beauty but predominantly evil. Attempts to civilise him have failed and so we feel that he is not fully human.

One particular way in which man expresses his civilisation is through Art. Art is like nurture because it takes natural elements and forms them into something of greater power, beauty and significance. Art also imposes order on disorder and through it man shapes his environment and gives ordered expression to his ideas. Because there are obvious parallels and similarities between *nurture*, *civilisation* and *Art*, each can be an analogy of the other in relation to Nature. *The Tempest* explores these concepts in fascinating ways.

Shakespeare uses the idea of Nature in two ways in *The Tempest*: on the one hand there is the view of the primitive, possibly derived from Montaigne (see 2.2. (b)) which says that a natural society without all the accretions of 'civilisation' would be a happy one; on the other hand there is the suggestion that something natural is imperfect and in need of refinement through Art. Caliban's closeness to Nature is emphasised by his great speeches in Act I, scene ii (331-45) and II.ii. (161-74) where he reveals an intimate knowledge of and association with all the island's natural life and resources. However, Prospero and Miranda find Caliban sadly lacking in what they see as normal requirements:

> I pitied thee,
> Took pains to make thee speak, taught thee each hour
> One thing or another. When thou didst not, savage,
> Know thine own meaning, but wouldst gabble like
> A thing most brutish. (i.ii. 354-8)

This educative process, in which both Prospero and Miranda play a part, shows nurture shaping the imperfect creation of Nature. The failure of the enterprise is summed up in Prospero's outburst:

> A devil, a born devil, on whose nature
> Nurture can never stick; (IV. 188-9)

and we feel in these and the ensuing lines Prospero's profound sense of failure and wasted energy. Part of the frustration comes from the fact that recollection of Caliban has interrupted the masque - the fullest demonstration of Art. Art has not succeeded in refining Caliban; even his response to music has been a primitive, almost animal reaction. By contrast, centuries of tradition in Art have produced wisdom and refinement in the courtiers. They are capable of witty discourse, a fine appreciation of music, an awareness of theatre, though, sadly, Anthonio has benefited less than Caliban. Prospero can only describe *him* as 'unnatural' (V. i. 79), devoid even of the basic gifts of Nature.

Shakespeare, like all great dramatists, poses the moral questions but leaves his audiences to seek for answers. At no point in the play is the cultivated teacher, Prospero, more unattractive than in the moment when he orders the spirits who have just performed the masque to become hounds to hunt Caliban and his crew. His fury and resort to violent tactics are, so records tell us, reminiscent of the way that invading Spaniards treated natives of the West Indies.

By contrast with the failure of Caliban's education, Miranda's education has taken a person already gifted by Nature with beauty and sweetness and fashioned a human being of genuine worth. The purpose of civilisation is to take *natural* elements and shape them into something better. In the case of Anthonio who has 'Expelled remorse and nature' (V. i. 76) civilisation has failed: he lacks compassion and family affinity, two of the most 'natural' properties of mankind. In his rage, Prospero appears to behave little better but finally he fights against the 'natural' reaction of revenge and offers forgiveness.

Ferdinand and Miranda represent the finest of the products of Nature and Art. Miranda, because of her isolation from the civilised world, has been untarnished by its intrigues: her innocence is both attractive and idealised. Ferdinand, brought up as a courtier, has acquired the gentility and refinement which such an education *should* produce. They both fall prey to the most natural of emotions but, unlike Caliban, Ferdinand is able to employ the self-discipline and restraint that decorum demands. The relationship, therefore, is transformed above the level of physical lust, to a refined courtship.

In a similar way, the artist also takes 'natural' unspoilt elements – sounds, movement, colours – refining and shaping them. This ordering of what may be natural disorder is shown by Prospero in the development of what he calls 'my so potent Art' (V. i. 50). In the speech from which those words are taken he explains how he has controlled the natural elements and used them for his purpose. Yet much of the control Prospero exercises over his enemies is through the media of music and theatre; recall how Sebastian describes the appearance of the banquet as 'A living drollery' (III. iii. 21) and how its disappearance is really an elaborate theatrical trick. This, of course, is not the only time when we see Prospero as an artist of the theatre and the finest demonstration of his Art is the presentation of the masque. So, throughout the play in which the magician shapes the events and finally renounces his Art, we are reminded of the art of the playwright, creating words, images and events – taking the variety of natural experience and fashioning it into a play. Prospero represents Art as Caliban represents one aspect of Nature. Not only has Prospero found the means to control Nature in the broadest sense, he has, through temperance and self-discipline, largely controlled his *own* nature. The play seems to be saying that anything we can describe as 'natural' is often a beautiful, always a potent and sometimes a dangerous force which may need shaping by man. The gifts of Art and civilisation help him to achieve this.

4.6 APPEARANCE AND REALITY

By the conclusion of the first scene of *The Tempest* the audience and Miranda think that they have seen a ship lost at sea. This opening scene is often considered to be very 'realistic' compared with other more fanciful scenes and yet, by the end of the play we can confirm Prospero's claim that there was no shipwreck and no-one was drowned. The reality of that opening scene turns out to be an 'insubstantial pageant' and the outcome the precise opposite of what it appeared to be.

One of the features of the play is that the characters, all more or less in Prospero's power, become increasingly uncertain as to the borders between appearance and reality. Gonzalo persists in pointing out that their clothes show no signs of having been soaked in the sea, as if, perhaps, their swim to land had been an illusion. As the play progresses, Gonzalo is prepared to believe the strange visions that he has seen, while even the cynical Sebastian is convinced by the vision of the banquet that there are far more fantastic things in the world than he had once admitted. The effect of the experiences of the island on all the courtiers is to confuse, disorientate and trouble them so that they no longer know what they believe or what is illusion and what reality.

Shakespeare presents the theme in a complex way so that there is a danger that in trying to isolate it you gain the impression of a neatly worked-out scheme on the part of the playwright. In fact, Shakespeare allows the ideas of appearance and reality to permeate the entire play; but there are four particularly noticeable and often interrelated facets.

Deception
It is only when Gonzalo and Alonso fall asleep that the complete nature of Anthonio and Sebastian emerges. Masquerading as loyal subjects, they encourage the king to sleep while they stand guard (II.i. 192-9). It soon becomes apparent that they are treacherous opportunists who will take advantage of the situation to seize power illegally. Similarly, Stephano and Trinculo deceive Caliban into thinking they are gods in order to further

their own violent ends; yet they also deceive themselves into thinking that their scheme is realistic. The most painful moments for all the characters are those when they are confronted with the truth about themselves and their sin is exposed to others.

Magic

Prospero the magician manipulates events so that all the other characters enter a maze of increasing complexity. Their experiences all seem vividly real and painful but, in the end, the causes of their sufferings turn out to be largely illusory. The point of this, as the critic Alvin Kernan puts it, is that 'The world is stranger than man thinks and the experiences of the moment, no matter how intense, lose their reality in the miraculous process of change and transformation through which all life passes'. Prospero relies largely on magic to achieve his ends: he and Ariel appear and disappear at will; visions affect all the characters. Under the impression that his father is drowned, Ferdinand is charmed by music and thinks Miranda a goddess; Miranda thinks him a spirit. Alonso, convinced that his son is drowned, sees visions of strange spirits but finally confronts reality in the 'vision' of Ferdinand and Miranda united in love. Stephano and Trinculo are tricked by appearances and sounds, coming finally to reality at the end of the play, when even Caliban recognises them for what they are.

Theatre

Theatre is a total illusion which the audience agrees to share with the actors. This works on many levels. Shakespeare's verse is easily accepted as 'real' speech; an empty stage can represent an island; three hours can stand for several days.; actors are not their 'real' selves. Much of the magic Prospero uses takes the form of theatre. A contemporary list of theatre properties shows that theatre companies in Shakespeare's time possessed a table with a reversible top and an artificial banquet attached to it. This not only explains how the disappearance of the banquet in *The Tempest* was achieved but also why the table itself disappears at a later stage direction (see III. iii.) It is one of several practical examples of theatrical illusions within the play and when Prospero describes the masque as a 'vanity' he may be suggesting that it really lacks substance. So ultimately do the shipwreck and the fears of Alonso and Ferdinand; thus the boundaries between tangible fact and theatrical fiction are deliberately vague and shifting.

Dreams

When Prospero says 'We are such stuff/As dreams are made on' (IV. i. 156-7) he is suggesting that our lives are of the same uncertain blend of appearance and reality as a dream or play. In some respects *The Tempest* has dream-like qualities reinforced by the important moments when characters fall asleep and by the powerful image of waking from a dream which dominates the final scene of reunion.

Miranda falls asleep during her father's discourse; the mariners, we are told by Ariel, remain asleep in their ship throughout the main action of the play and when Alonso and Gonzalo are overcome with sleep Sebastian and Anthonio's immediate discussion centres upon whether or not they are dreaming (II.i. 210-218); Prospero sleeps every afternoon and Caliban describes his own dreaming in graphic terms (III.ii. 140-5). Just as in a dream strange events, shapes and sounds seem real, so in *The Tempest* fantasy and reality appear to interchange. Caliban cries to 'dream again' because the imaginary world of the dream seems preferable to the real world. It is when that ugly real world intrudes into the mind of Prospero, that the masque – the illusion – comes to an end. The end of the masque is sudden and abrupt but elsewhere Prospero uses the word 'dissolve' (IV. i. 154) as an image of the process by which the worlds of appearance and reality usually move from one to another almost perceptibly. That image is repeated in (V. i. 64) when he describes the returning consciousness of Gonzalo and Alonso together with other members of the court. Ferdinand feels as though 'my spirits, as in a dream, are all bound up' (I.ii. 489) and he only emerges into reality as the charms under which he has fallen gradually give way; he realises that Miranda *is* his betrothed and his is reunited with Alonso.

4.7 EXPLORATION AND COLONISATION

As we have seen in 2.2 Shakespeare was writing at a time when many hazardous, speculative sea-voyages were being undertaken. The reality and topicality of these voyages is vividly brought home in Ariel's description of St Elmo's fire (I.ii. 200) 'the still-vexed Bermoothes' – the endlessly stormy Bermudas (I.ii. 229) and the whole account of the storm and miraculous escape. No wonder Gonzalo is forced to remark:

> Our hint of woe
> Is common; every day some sailor's wife,
> The masters of some merchant, and the merchant
> Have just our theme of woe; (II.i. 3-6)

Travellers' tales which filtered back home contained elements of fact and fantasy. Such tales are referred to by Gonzalo when he says:

> When we were boys
> Who would believe that there were mountaineers
> Dew-lapped like bulls, whose throats had hanging at 'em
> Wallets of flesh? Or that there were such men
> Whose heads stood in their breasts? (III.iii. 43-7)

Accounts of the strange inhabitants of remote islands, especially the West Indies, certainly influenced Trinculo's and Stephano's initial reactions to Caliban. Trinculo (II.ii. 18-42) is quite prepared to believe that Caliban is a monster with four legs or even a fish-like creature but Stephano, although also thinking he has four legs, immediately assumes that Caliban belongs to the 'savages and men of Ind' (II.ii. 59). Trinculo has already mentioned the fascination of Europeans with 'Indians' when he jokes that Caliban would make him a fortune if he were exhibited in England, as was the custom as the time (II.ii. 30-4). In the face of the evidence provided by 'Indians' brought to Europe there was still an uneasy mixture of truth and fable. Sebastian finds that the island is changing his perception:

> Now I will believe
> That there are unicorns; that in Arabia
> There is one tree, the phoenix' throne, one phoenix
> At this hour reigning there. (III.iii. 21-4)

Anthonio is equally convinced that the travellers' tales are true:

> Travellers ne'er did lie,
> Though fools at home condemn 'em. (III.iii. 26-7)

and Gonzalo shows how the island has convinced him of things which would never be believed at home:

> If in Naples
> I should report this now, would they believe me?
> If I should say I saw such islanders (III.iii. 28-9)

With great skill Shakespeare has taken the relatively simple subject of travellers' tales and used it to create one of his recurring themes – that of the contrast between illusion and reality. The uncertain boundaries between the two concepts also lie at the root of the dream-like quality of much of the play and the ease with which Sebastian and Anthonio are prepared to suggest that they hear lions roaring (see II.i. 311-7) and Caliban is ready to accept that Stephano has 'dropped from heaven' (ii.ii. 139-41).

Elizabethan and Jacobean mariners sailing for the New World (the 'brave new world' of Miranda has particular meaning) cherished the half-belief and hope that they might discover lands where the Golden Age of innocence still existed, or could be recreated. Gonzalo has this vision for a 'commonwealth' that would 'excel the Golden Age' and articulates it in Act II, scene i (149-69). The drift of his argument is that violence, corruption and therefore the necessity for law would be unknown in a state where Nature operated her own laws. The original inhabitants of such a land may well be the 'noble savages' of whom Montaigne had written (see 2.2. (b)) but the newcomers inevitably become colonialists. Not only were travellers in search of a new world, they came to exploit it. Caliban has no doubt that the island is his:

> This island's mine by Sycorax my mother,
> Which thou tak'st from me. (I.ii. 332-3)

and he goes on to explain how he had shown Prospero the colonialist all the resources of the island in return for initial kindness. Caliban repeats the entire process for Stephano (II.ii. 150 onwards), responding once again to newcomers' rather condescending generosity. Prospero had 'stroked' Caliban and Stephano given him drink. This attitude of the settlers who had both eventually made Caliban their slave (see I.ii. 312-14 and II.ii. 186) was exaggerated to the point of distortion in Dr Jonathan Miller's production of the play and described in an interview with David Hirst in 1983 (see Further Reading):

> the play represents the tragic and inevitable disintegration of more primitive culture as the result of European invasion and colonisation ... Prospero's effect was deleterious ... disinheriting those who have a close connection with nature ... The comic scenes ... based on the image of British private soldiers in Port Said, making the natives drunk, patronising and bullying them; it is what army sergeants ... always do when they arrive in a foreign country ... they shout loudly at the people to make them understand, make them drunk and then get drunk themselves. (p.50)

Miller's interpretation however, helped to make sense of the fact that Prospero, rather like a colonial governor-general, is both somewhat irritable and dictatorial. His presence on the island demands that Caliban, its native inhabitant, complies with *his* wishes and standards. Caliban's lust and his primitive religion are regarded as evil but, paradoxically, Prospero depends on Caliban's service for survival. Prospero also exacts constant and loyal service from Ariel as a payment for his having rescued him from Sycorax's imprisonment. This original act of kindness and humanity is rapidly exploited by Prospero once he recognises what a powerful agent Ariel can be.

Stephano and Trinculo are also quick to play upon Caliban's credibility, allowing him to think that they are gods. Caliban understands the world in terms of natural resources, local spirits and the white man – Prospero – who has a more powerful form of magic than he has ever encountered. As with many settlers, this knowledge sometimes takes the form of superior scientific knowledge and of a literary-based culture: the first thing which Prospero teaches Caliban is *language* and Caliban sees Prospero's magic as emanating from his *books*. Prospero fails to 'westernise' Caliban but Shakespeare does not always present a particularly attractive view of the world to which Prospero intends to return once he has confronted his enemies. It is corrupt and potentially violent although enjoying sophisticated forms of art and manners. The new arrivals to the island have brought their decorum, the music and dancing but also their intrigues and vices. It is as if a new world of innocence will immediately be corrupted by 'civilised' man. On the other hand Shakespeare seems to be pointing to the attitude of early missionaries who, according to sources available to him, felt compelled both to convert and exploit the natives, using such skills as making dams to catch fish (see Caliban's song at the end of Act II, scene ii) to assist in their survival.

5 TECHNIQUES

5.1 CHARACTERS AND CHARACTERISATION

It is only possible to say anything of value about the characters in a play when their words, actions and motives have been thoroughly examined. It is a good idea to try reading the scenes through from the point of view of *each* of the characters in turn, considering not only what they say but also what they are doing when they are *not* speaking. This will provide insights into what actors call the 'subtext' – the drives and concerns which lie beneath what a character says.

The characters in *The Tempest* do not present the profound psychological insights of, say, the great tragedies but this does not diminish their interest. An initial consideration of the characters reveals that their *names* alone, are fascinating and significant. Shakespeare creates a number of puns and anagrams on these names; take, for example, Ferdinand's response to learning Miranda's name:

> Admired Miranda,
> Indeed the top of admiration, (III.i. 37–8)

and Sebastian's grim pun 'we prosper well in our return' (II.i. 73) or the obvious derivation of Caliban from Cannibal. Much of the interest of the play is generated by the meetings between the various characters and the consequences that ensue. Many interesting views of the characters themselves can also be gained by discovering how actors and actresses have portrayed them.

Prospero
Prospero is generally reckoned to be one of the most difficult parts in Shakespeare and many famous actors have preferred to play Caliban. Critical opinions of him range from 'tedious and bad-tempered' to 'com-

passionate mage':- part wise man, part magician. Such divergence of views is caused by the complexity of his character and the doubt surrounding the precise nature of his aims. The most obvious characteristic of Prospero is his total domination of the action – in a play of just over 2000 lines he speaks approximately one third of them himself. However, if we look at the scenes in which he appears he monopolises every conversation and holds the stage on his own to a quite remarkable extent. The events of the play all relate to his activities and he is single-minded in pursuit of his ends.

Prospero is different things to different people: to Miranda he is 'dearest father'; to Ariel 'Master', 'commander' 'grave sir'; to Caliban 'the tyrant'; to Ferdinand 'composed of harshness'. All these labels emphasise Prospero's authority and it is certainly true that he is dictatorial. Two factors must be considered alongside this image, however. First, the nature of the experience he went through at the time of his usurpation and second the short time he has in which to achieve so much. Both factors make him determined not to fail in his endeavours and impatient of obstacles.

Prospero is, in a sense, Renaissance man – embracing all knowledge, anxious to understand and control the natural world, finding a new self-confidence. He is the Artist, shaping events, creating illusions. He is the well-read magician, dabbling in Divinity. In the end he shows in his tears his compassion for his suffering fellow-men but his own self-discipline hardly cracks. By any standards he is strictly moral and sees it as his duty to impose such standards on others. Much loved by his people, he was nevertheless too unaware of the effect of his gradual retreat from public life and that fatal error of judgement set in motion all the events which followed.

It is also possible to see in the character of Prospero a representation of God. In Shakespeare's day the *Bible* in English was becoming more widely available and people were taking an increasing interest in the idea of God as active in the affairs of men as revealed in the *Old Testament*. God, the supreme dramatist of the cosmos, can in some ways be paralleled by Prospero with his island as a microcosm of the universe. He leads his erring people through guilt, contrition and repentance to salvation. He is seen as benign yet terrible. You should give serious thought to the idea of the play as a Christian allegory (that is, a story with a symbolic meaning).

Alonso

Alonso is the first person to speak to the mariners in the storm but he is quickly reminded that the elements are no respecters of royal rank and he goes to his prayers without further words in that scene. His second appearance in the play is also notable for the brevity of his comments and the lengthy silences during which he agonises over the loss of his son. By contrast with the small impact his personal appearances make early in the play, we learn a good deal about him by report. Prospero explains that Alonso, for reasons which are not explained, was already his enemy when the plot to supplant him was hatched with Anthonio; Alonso stood to benefit greatly and the ultimate responsibility for Prospero's sorrow lay with him (see I.ii. 121-30). Ariel and Prospero constantly refer to 'the King's ship' and 'the King's son' while Ariel, prophetically, sings to Ferdinand that his father must suffer 'a sea change'.

The process of that change involves Alonso first in fear, then depression and ultimately despair and resignation before he eventually finds what he has lost. He seems weak, too weary to react to the impudence of Anthonio and Sebastian, easily swayed to partake of the banquet. Yet he has to live with his guilt and it is he whom Ariel, dressed as a harpy, addresses most directly and he whose conscience sends rushing suicidally from the stage only to reappear (see Act V) 'with a frantic gesture'. Alonso (V. i. 71) is the first of Prospero's enemies to be confronted directly but we are never allowed to forget that he *is* king. Gonzalo is praised for his loyalty to him and it is Alonso's displeasure with which Prospero threatens Anthonio and Sebastian.

The final impression of Alonso is one of considerable dignity. He craves forgiveness, reveals an awareness of the supernatural powers that have been at work and presides over the joy of Ferdinand and Miranda with great tenderness. Of all the characters in the play he has made the longest spiritual journey and undergone the greatest change.

Miranda

Miranda's first words are compassionate and she remains the epitome of sweetness. Her attitude to life is unquestioning and undemanding. In spite of her distant memories of childhood she seems to have been remarkably happy on the island and it is Prospero who is aware that the time has come for her to enlarge her experience and leave parental care. Miranda is a symbol of innocence (which she calls 'plain and holy') and of beauty (note the various references to her physical appearance). She represents the product of a successful education and a loving relationship with her parent. Much of our fascination with Miranda comes from the gradual way in which she defies and yet retains her love for her father. Miranda is *not* naive, she has learned from all her experiences and her unfortunate incident with Caliban has not soured her attitude: this is a tribute to her father's care.

Caliban

As you will see from the section on critical responses, many performers and commentators have found Caliban to be the most intriguing character in the play and among Shakespeare's most remarkable creations. The playwright has amalgamated a number of contemporary myths and ideas into a single character. Caliban is partly the 'wild man' of travellers' tales and journals, partly the deformed child of a sinful union. In an age that was largely unsympathetic to physical handicap, any kind of deformity was thought of as a curse on parentage. As Caliban's parents were a witch and the devil he is scarcely human and partially evil spirit. He is, however, earthbound (Prospero calls him 'thou earth, thou!') and shows great familiarity with the natural environment. Being brutish he is initially without language but a nobler side of his nature emerges as he demonstrates his usage of words. Most of the important features of Caliban's character have emerged in our consideration of the scenes in which he appears; these should be studied carefully as they are essential to a total understanding of the play.

Ariel
Ariel underlines the fact that he is a spirit in his remark to Prospero 'Mine would, sir, were I human' (V. i. 19). Prospero replies:

> Hast thou, which art but air, a touch, a feeling
> Of their afflictions,

suggesting that this airy spirit does not generally feel emotions. We see, however, that Ariel can be moody, anxious to please, exultant and mischievous. He is something of a showman: his descriptions of his own achievements read like elaborate stage directions (see I.ii. 195-206 or IV. i. 171-84 for example) and he confronts the guilty courtiers like a performer, dressed as a harpy – the symbol of vengeance. Indeed, Ariel is the chief performer in the drama shaped by Prospero. He is able to change his shape or become invisible, he is a practical joker and, because he so desires his freedom, anxious to please his master. Prospero calls him 'fine apparition', 'My quaint Ariel', 'fine spirit', 'my delicate Ariel', 'fine Ariel' and flatters the spirit for his performance:

> Bravely the figure of this harpy hast thou
> Performed, my Ariel; a grace it had devouring. (III.iii. 83-4)

Ariel, in turn draws attention to the speed and skill with which he acts (see IV. i. 45-7) and there is a strange and wonderful moment when we sense Ariel's feeling of insecurity:

> ARIEL Do you love, master? No?
> PROSPERO Dearly, my delicate Ariel.

and Prospero's dependence upon his servant spirit. In calling him 'my tricksy spirit' at one point Prospero also emphasises the contemporary idea of spirits as jokers who plague people. Stephano and Trinculo have good reason to hold this view of Ariel. Ariel's songs stress the ethereal quality of the spirit; air bringing 'sweet airs' – he is Prospero's chief agent of magic and without him the project would fail.

Gonzalo

We have three main views of Gonzalo in the play. The first is Prospero's view, so favourable that Miranda exclaims 'Would I might/But ever see that man' (I.ii. 169). In Prospero's eyes, Gonzalo is 'noble', 'good', 'holy', 'honourable' and his 'true preserver'; his main qualities are 'charity' and 'gentleness'. These opinions, expressed at various times in the play and communicated to Ariel and Miranda, are confirmed and enhanced by a second view – that of the audience.

The 'honest old Councillor', as he is described in the list of characters, invariably talks a great deal and usually speaks first in the scenes of epi-sodes in which he appears. His first appearance is typical of him: he urges patience, showing concern for the king and interest in other characters. His unselfishness and optimism are evident throughout the play; he never ceases trying to comfort Alonso; he urges his companions to see the bright side of their situation and rebukes Anthonio and Sebastian for their lack of gentleness (II.i. 139). It is Gonzalo who is filled with wonder at the fresh condition of the courtiers' clothes, who has the vision and imagination to speculate on a 'commonwealth' on the island or to accept the new ideas with which he is confronted (II. ii. 149-70 and III. iii. 43-9).

We see Gonzalo as entirely human. Sometimes he *does* talk too much; he is fatigued and needs rest (III.ii. 2); he weeps (V. i. 16); becomes confused (V. i. 104-6) and rejoices at restored harmony (V. i. 200-13). His great, moving, speeches of blessing and finality in Act V show that he alone has really understood what has taken place in the drama. Gonzalo's wisdom may sometimes be overlooked in his long-windedness but even more remarkable is his loyalty to Alonso. Prospero addresses Gonzalo in Act V as 'a loyal sir/To him thou follow'st' and throughout the play we are aware of this. Nevertheless, Gonzalo is perfectly clear as to the nature and guilt of the man to whom he is so loyal and it is only his sense of divinely ordained order that sustains him.

A third and very unsympathetic view of Gonzalo is projected by Anthonio and Sebastian. To them he is an irritant, an impediment and a target for cheap jibes. They cannot enter his world and he throws their wickedness and small-mindedness into relief. Gonzalo is Shakespeare's reminder that, even in a very corrupt world, human goodness is possible.

Ferdinand

Ferdinand does not appear in the play until well on into the second scene but the audience has already heard several specific references to him. In the storm he seems to be already at prayers and he is the first to leap overboard (see I.ii. 212-15) crying 'Hell is empty/And all the devils are here'. Ariel also gives a vivid picture of Ferdinand's behaviour on land (I.ii. 221-4) which evokes the image of a melancholic, courtly young man familiar to Shakespeare's audience in miniature portrait paintings. Later, Francisco presents his highly formalised account of Ferdinand's swim to land (II.i. 117-25). All these reports, together with Alonso's growing despair at ever finding his son, contribute to the sense of loss and eventual reunion which is central to the play's structure.

As a character, Ferdinand may seem almost too virtuous to modern eyes. He is idealised to the extent that he represents refinement and the best products of civilisation. His language and conduct have an absolute decorum. Ferdinand's predicament is that he thinks himself king but is more charmed than any other character: first he is charmed by music which numbs his sorrow and then he is charmed by Miranda so that anything else fades into insignificance (see I.ii. 489-96). He undergoes his trial with complete success, proving himself capable of self-discipline and coming to value Miranda, his prize, even more as a result. In uniting the family of Alonso with his own by the betrothal of Miranda to Ferdinand, Prospero ensures political harmony and a hopeful future in the hands of attractive, responsible young people.

Anthonio and Sebastian

These are arguably the most unattractive characters in the play. With less excuse than Caliban they remain unchanged at the end even though they have been through purgation. The critic Theodore Spencer remarked that 'Anthonio is the rigid, selfish schemer. An egotistic isolationist, he is cut off from all concerns but his own'. However, he and his confederate Sebastian gain strength from each other as cowards so often do. In the opening scene we see them as loud-mouths and at their next appearance as insensitive beings who find pleasure in taunting. They are already considering how other people's misfortune can be turned to their own advantage. Dishonest and at times defiant this 'brace of lords' are traitors and can find no answer when they are confronted with their crimes. Prospero provides a great deal of information concerning Anthonio's original plot in his lengthy exposition to Miranda in Act I. You should study this carefully and then consider how Anthonio tempts Sebastian into murder and what his ultimate motives might be.

5.2   THE LANGUAGE

The words spoken by various characters and a few stage directions are the only elements which a playwright leaves us for the creation of his play. Language, therefore, has many functions in a text: it may provide essential information for the context of the play; it provides insights into the minds of the characters; it evokes mental images in the imaginations of the audience; it differentiates between the characters and it must be accepted by the audience as representing 'real' dialogue spoken by believable people.

Shakespeare's language in *The Tempest* shows the mature theatrical craftsman at his most relaxed and masterful. Though he writes in both verse and prose the variety he achieves in both is remarkable. At times verse and prose are virtually indistinguishable, there is highly 'poetic' prose and verse so subtle and flexible that it seems as natural as prose. In all, Shakespeare achieves what his more educated and courtly audience would understand by *decorum* - an aptness of every style to the subject matter and situation.

The range of language in *The Tempest* includes the earthy prose of the 'low' characters and the witty, punning chatter of Anthonio and Sebastian. Prose is also used for the violent naturalism of the storm; but just as that scene moves into verse at its final climax so Anthonio and Sebastian use the greater intensity of verse for their plotting. The transition to verse at line 109 in Act II, scene i. introduces a formal and elaborate form of discourse from Alonso, Francisco and Anthonio. Metaphors are never far from the surface here and the structure is complex yet elegant. The irony of this admirable mastery of language, the mark of sophistication and civilisation, is that it conceals malice or disguises deeply-felt emotions whereas Caliban's speeches, invariably in verse (even when in the company of Trinculo and Stephano) are far more rooted in reality and of more genuine worth and beauty. Indeed, one of the paradoxes of the play is that Caliban, who has only recently acquired language, speaks some of the finest lines in the play.

Most of the characters who speak in verse have their own characteristic style: Prospero's sometimes rather archaic, sometimes spell-like, always strong and sweeping in its scope; Miranda's, more tentative, economical and restrained; Ariel's almost breathless and rather showy - and so on. The accumulated power of Prospero's words comes home forcibly in his furious outburst at Ariel (I.ii. 50 onwards), his terrible punishment of Caliban (I.ii. 326-31) or his great invocation of spirits (V. i. 32-57). In such cases we find examples of Shakespeare's ability to evoke rich images with an apt phrase: 'To run upon the sharp wind of the north', 'Side stitches that shall pen thy breath up' or:

> 'twixt the green sea and the azured vault
> Set roaring war,

all produce powerful mental pictures. Even more remarkable is the effect often created by a single word: Prospero speaks of 'thy *crying* self', Caliban of 'a thousand *twangling* instruments' Ariel of 'my *potent* master'. This verbal magic is appropriate for a play in which spells abound. Much of the language creates an atmosphere of strangeness; its pace is often slow and dreamlike and there are references to both the natural and imaginary universe.

The basic Shakespearean verse line is of ten syllables – a decasyllabic line – and is unrhymed. This 'blank verse' line is normally an 'iambic pentameter', that is, a line of ten syllables divided into five 'feet' each of which is an iamb consisting of an unstressed syllable ($\cup$) followed by a stressed syllable (-). The lines were designed to be spoken so that the natural stresses of everyday speech provide the rhythm, for example:

> For this, be sure tonight thou shalt have cramps
> $\cup$ -/ $\cup$ -/ $\cup$ -/ $\cup$ -/ $\cup$ - /

Sometimes a line will be divided between two speakers but its rhythmic structure remains the same, for example:

> PROSPERO   What is't thou canst demand?
> ARIEL $\cup$ -/ $\cup$ -/ $\cup$ -/   My liberty
> $\cup$-/$\cup$-/

Obviously a play consisting entirely of iambic pentameters would become very tedious and would certainly not convey the illusion of 'real' speech. Shakespeare therefore makes frequent variations from the basic, underlying pattern. *The Tempest* contains a considerable number of 'hypermetric' lines, that is lines with an extra syllable or two, for example

> On their sustaining garments not a blemish

or

> Being capable of all ill I pitied thee

You will notice also that these examples include minor changes to the metrical structure – the first ends with a 'spondee' – two stressed syllables together – whereas the second begins with a trochee (-$\cup$), the reverse of an iamb. The 'substitution' of one kind of foot for another or the 'inversion' of a foot to its opposite are all part of the technique for liberating and vitalising the verse, thus sustaining our interest.

In *The Tempest*, more than any of his earlier plays, Shakespeare uses the basic form of blank verse as a flexible medium. Most noticeable are the constant 'enjambments', where the sense flows from one line to another and often over several lines. Very few lines are 'end-stopped', their natural pause falling at the conclusion of the line; the 'caesura' more often falling in the middle of lines. A glance at the punctuation will reveal the dynamic, forward movement of the verse and will sometimes expose 'anacolutha', unfinished sentences, which in *spoken* language are frequently more common than rounded sentences. The remarkable naturalism thus achieved is contrasted with the stately formality of the masque or of Ferdinand's wooing of Miranda. Here, especially, we can see the power of other technical devices such as *alliteration* and *repetition*:

> But you, O you,
> So perfect and so peerless, are created
> Of every creature's best. (III.i. 46-8)

you should search the text for the many other examples.

It is impossible to divorce the consideration of the *language* of the play from any of its other elements; it contributes to every aspect. In Ferdinand's lines we catch the *mood* of the moment and its pace: these words cannot be spoken quickly or insincerely for example. *The Tempest* is particularly rich in puns, vivid and colourful descriptions, evocations of sounds – all these contribute to the action of the play, the distinctiveness of the characters or a sense of dramatic irony. Imagery is created through the words and the language is sometimes enriched by music – all these features contribute to the total theatrical experience.

As further examples of the techniques we have been considering let us take two short passages which demonstrate Shakespeare's flexible use of blank verse. The first is taken from Act I:

> PROSPERO My brother and thy uncle, called Anthonio –   66
> I pray thee mark me, that a brother should
> Be so perfidious – he, whom next thyself
> Of all the world I loved, and to him put
> The manage of my state, as at that time
> Through all the signories it was the first,
> And Prospero the prime duke, being so reputed

In dignity, and for the liberal arts
Without a parallel; those being all my study,
The government I cast upon my brother,
And to my state grew stranger, being transported
And rapt in secret studies. Thy false uncle –
Dost thou attend me?   78

The sentence which Prospero begins 'my brother and thy uncle' (66) is never concluded. The distress which the memory of this act of treachery gives Prospero causes his syntax to break down and this line is an *anacoluthon*. The erratic flow of the lines is achieved partly by irregular numbers of syllables to the lines – only lines 67, 69, 70, 71 and 73 have ten syllables, the remainder are *hypermetric* with eleven, twelve and even thirteen syllables. Only line 75 is *end-stopped* in the sense that it is a complete unit of thought with a short pause before and after; all the remaining lines are examples of *enjambment* where the sense continues either without break from the previous line or straight on to the next.

By contrast Ferdinand's words to Miranda in Act. III, scene i (37–42) are restrained and stately:

FERDINAND   Admired Miranda,
        Indeed the top of admiration, worth
        What's dearest to the world! Full many a lady
        I have eyed with best regard, and many a time   40
        Th' harmony of their tongues hath into bondage
        Brought my too diligent ear.

Ferdinand begins with a *pun*, gently playing on Miranda's name and remarking that, as both words imply 'wonderful', she is aptly named. He emphasises his feelings with the alliteration of 'worth', 'What's' and 'world' but the uninterrupted flow of his praise is enhanced by the enjambments. Notice that the *caesura* invariably occurs near the middle of lines rather than at the end. You should compare this with some of the very formal verse spoken in the masque (IV. i. 60–138) where many of the lines are *end-stopped*. There are many more whole, rounded sentences in Ferdinand's speech than in our example from Prospero's. This befits the nature of Ferdinand's purpose at this time but notice how Shakespeare still slips in the odd additional syllable to break the regular pattern.

5.3 THE IMAGE OF THE SEA

When a playwright uses a word or visual effect to suggest *more* than the mere literal or commonplace meaning he is creating an 'image'. Imagery provides rich dimensions of meaning and can suggest related themes and new ideas; a single image can evoke many kinds of associations and provide a satisfying artistic experience for the audience by its appeal to the mind. An image is really the representation of an idea: what is seen and heard on stage has deeper implications. On the surface *The Tempest* may seem an improbable and rather unsatisfactory tale, yet by clever use of imagery Shakespeare gives the play profound significance and stimulates our imaginations. The predominant image of the play is the sea.

The sea surrounds *The Tempest* as it does an island. The play begins with a storm and ends with calm seas but almost every scene contains reminders that the characters are on an island with the sounds, sights and smells of the ever-present sea. The sea represents a supernatural force greater than man. At times it seems to be under Prospero's direct control: Miranda thinks that he has 'Put the wild waters in this roar' (I.ii. 2) and Prospero says that he has

> called forth the mutinous winds
> And twixt the green sea and the azured vault
> Set roaring war: (V. i. 42–4)

but it appears that Prospero co-operates with Divine powers, for Ariel describes how 'Jove's lightning' and 'most mighty Neptune' (i.ii. 201–4) were involved in the storm and later he reveals to the courtiers that it was Destiny which had caused 'the never-surfeited sea' to cast them onto the island (III.iii. 53). The sea-god Neptune also personifies the sea in Prospero's great invocation (V. i. 35).

The sea is an agent of great potency which affects each character differently. Ariel, though a spirit of the air, is also a 'nymph o' the sea' (I. ii. 302) who has been privileged to 'tread the ooze of the salt deep' (I. ii. 252) and who has actually helped in the making of the storm; but for Trinculo the prospect of another storm is simply a vision of 'a foul bombard that would shed his liquor' (II.ii. 21) – an extension of his own drunkenness. Alonso feels that the sea 'mocks' him (III.iii. 9) and in a powerful image of the sounds of the sea and the texture of the sea-bed he is reminded by the sea of his terrible loss (III.iii. 95–102).

Perhaps the most poignant images of the sea are contained within the mysterious expressions 'sea-sorrow' (I.ii. 170) and 'sea-change' (i.ii. 402). For Prospero there have really been two tempests: the first, remembered bitterly in his long narrative to Miranda, is the cause of the second:

> There they hoist us,
> To cry to the sea, that roared to us; to sigh
> To the winds, whose pity sighing back again
> Did us but loving wrong. (I.ii. 148–51)

A similar fate had, of course, befallen Sycorax (see I.ii. 271). In almost every description of the later tempest there is mention of the roaring of the sea. Exposure of Prospero and Miranda to that cruel sea is the accusation Ariel hurls at the 'three men of sin' when the mock feast disappears; Ariel's use of the expression 'never-surfeited sea' evokes the fearsome appetite of the ocean. So, as part of Prospero's project, the courtiers are themselves 'sea-swallowed' as Anthonio puts it (II.i. 252) and they face their own sea-sorrow. For Alonso and Ferdinand this means a sense of profound loss and Ferdinand expresses this in another marine image, speaking of his eyes 'never since at ebb' (I.ii. 438). Ironically Prospero makes him drink sea-water as part of his punishment. Ferdinand's heroic struggle against the power of the sea is described, with some hyperbole, by Francisco in Act II (II. i. 117-25) but like Ferdinand, who has been

> Sitting on a bank
> Weeping again the king my father's wrack (I.ii. 391-2)

Alonso refuses to be comforted. Francisco's speech is provided with an ironic echo in the bravado of Stephano who assures Trinculo that 'For my part the sea cannot drown me; I swam, ere I could recover the shore, five-and-thirty leagues off and on' (III.ii. 13-15). Like Trinculo, who 'Swum ashore man, like a duck' (II.iii. 130), Stephano uses most of his references to the sea as images for drink. Although the sea has overwhelmed neither of them, drink certainly has!

   Shakespeare was too accurate an observer to represent the sea only as a threatening force. The same sea that roars can also lap benignly on the shore of the island. The divine forces represented by the sea are not solely concerned with revenge or sorrow. In the end Ferdinand is brought to realise that

> Though the seas
> threaten, they are merciful. (V. i. 177-8)

The sea has brought about a change in every character or his situation. The beautiful song in which Ariel introduces this idea (I.ii. 398-404) speaks of transformation and we have seen how Prospero effects this as part of his project. Anthonio and Sebastian, who had earlier used a sea-image for plotting:

SEB	Well, I am standing water.
ANTH	I'll teach you how to flow.
SEB	Do so. To ebb
	Hereditary sloth instructs me (II.i. 222-4)

are confronted with and forgiven their sin by Prospero. As they are made slowly aware of their misdeeds, Prospero uses an elaborate metaphor which once again evokes the tide and the sand:

> Their understanding
> Begins to swell, and the approaching tide
> Will shortly fill the reasonable shore,
> That now lies foul and muddy. (V. i. 79-82)

5.4 MUSIC AND DANCING

There are more specific instructions for music in the original text and stage directions of *The Tempest* than in any other play by Shakespeare. A production of the play without music is incomplete. To some extent this reflects the changing tastes in favour of a more spectacular kind of theatrical entertainment at the end of Shakespeare's career but music provides an element of magic that no other medium can rival and the dramatist exploits this to the full. We know that Shakespeare's company invariably included accomplished musicians, of whom at least one would be a boy-singer capable of playing the part of Ariel.

The music of *The Tempest* is of three main types: magic songs, instrumental music accompanying the action and bawdy songs. Ariel's three magic songs 'Come unto these yellow sands' (I.ii. 376-8), 'Full fathom five' (I.ii. 398-477) and 'Where the bee sucks' (V. i. 88-94) would almost certainly have been accompanied by the lute. Lute song was an art-form in which England led the world in Shakespeare's time and W. H. Auden has pointed out how uniquely suited for setting to music are the words of these songs, with their many single-syllable words. Fortunately a number of very early musical settings of these songs have survived and we can therefore have a fairly accurate idea of how they might have sounded in performance.

We have settings of 'Where the bee sucks' and 'Full fathom five' by Shakespeare's contemporary Robert Johnson (b. 1582) preserved in John Wilson's 1659 collection of *Cheerfull Ayres or Ballads*. Robert Johnson was a celebrated lutenist frequently associated with the court and the King's Men, and it is a reasonable assumption that these two airs were used at the first productions of the play. Some music by Johnson, possibly for the masque, has also been discovered in a manuscript in the British Museum; this gives a fair indication of the kind of instrumental music used in Shakespeare's day. Caliban sums up the situation when he says

> The isle is full of noises,
> Sounds and sweet airs (III.ii. 138-9)

Most of these 'solemn airs' are used to represent Prospero's magic. In Shakespeare's theatre they would probably have been played by unseen musicians on stringed instruments of the viol family. Ariel also plays on a pipe and tabor but we accept that he, too, is invisible. Examples of such music occur in Act I, scene II (376) where Ferdinand is convinced that 'these airs' are associated with Miranda whom he considers a goddess; Act II, scene, i (185) where the music induces sleep; Act II, scene i (301) when Ariel wakes Gonzalo; Act III, scene ii (128) where Ariel tricks Stephano and Trinculo; Act III, scene iii (16) as an accompaniment to the vision of a banquet and later at line 82 with the disappearance of the table; at intervals throughout the masque in Act IV: and in Act V, scene i (52) where the 'heavenly music' takes the form of a 'solemn air' to cure the disturbed brains of Prospero's enemies and Gonzalo. You should study each of these occurrences of music very carefully, examining its effect and then comparing these reactions with Caliban's speech (III.ii. 138 onwards). Once you have seen how music permeates the play you will appreciate the impact of Ariel's words 'they smelt music' (IV. i. 178).

The drunken songs of Stephano, Trinculo and Caliban are little better than the other noises with which the play abounds. From the first sounds of thunder and the Master's whistle to the howling of hounds in pursuit of the clowns, the play is a patchwork of discordant din. The harmony, an exact opposite to discord, is a quality which gradually prevails, affecting all but the most insensitive characters. Even Stephano appreciates the wonder of a kingdom where 'I shall have my music for nothing ' (III.ii. 148).

A particular sort of harmony is symbolised in the music of the masque. Although no original musical settings of the songs in the masque have survived we have sufficient evidence from similar entertainments of the time to know that the singing and incidental music played a most important part in the presentation. The moment when the goddess Iris enters to soft music has been beautifully foreshadowed in Act I when 'airs' accompany the first appearance of the 'goddess' Miranda, to whom Ferdinand is now betrothed. In the masque, as in Act III, scene iii, the music is also vital as an accompaniment for dancing which is a symbol of celebration and unity.

In neither case where dancing is specified in the play can we be certain what precise style and steps were envisaged and it remains a challenge to the modern choreographer to interpret the spirit of the original. The ritual, magical and 'weightless' qualities of dance are of significance in a performance.

With so many references to music and dancing as agents of Prospero's magic it is small wonder that many composers and choreographers have produced works for inclusion in *The Tempest*. Styles tend to reflect the tastes of the age in which the play is being produced. The songs, particularly 'Come unto these yellow sands' with its strange echo chorus, 'Full fathom five' with its wonderful alliteration and magical imagery and 'Where the bee sucks' so full of evocative ideas of freedom, have all attracted composers, some of whom have set the songs for independent use.

The Tempest has twice been transformed into an opera: once in 1674 with music by John Bannister (1630-79) and again in modern times under the title of Der Sturm with music composed by Frank Martin (b. 1890). A new score was written by Henry Purcell (1658-95) for the 1674 version in the year of his death. Among the other famous and important composers to have written incidental music for The Tempest are: Dr Thomas Arne (1710-78); John Christopher Smith (1712-95); Hector Berlioz (1803-69), Peter Ilich Tchaikovsky (1840-93); Arthur Sullivan (1842-1900) who began his career as a serious composer with his music for The Tempest at the age of 20; Engelbert Humperdinck (1854-1921); Jean Sibelius (1865-1957); Arthur Honegger (1892-1955) and Michael Tippett (b. 1905). In addition, the play has been transformed into a ballet by leading choreographers on at least five occasions: by Jean Coralli (1779-1854) in Paris (1834); Filippo Taglioni (1777-1871) in London (1838); Fred Howard (b. 1946) in London (1964); Imre Eck (b. 1930) in Helsinki (1974) and very recently again in London by Glenn Tetley (b. 1926). In 1985, the English composer Keith Cole used characters from The Tempest as the basis for a suite of evocative pieces for wind instruments.

All the music mentioned here is well worth exploring, though the ballets tend to vanish beyond recall; that so much has been composed shows that for the creative artist The Tempest has qualities which offer a seemingly endless fund of inspiration. As a student of the play you must decide not only what these qualities are but also what kind of music and dance you consider appropriate to the playwright's intentions. In recent years the development of electronic music and sound effects has opened up new possibilities which, in some ways, come very close to Caliban's description of the mysterious sounds of the island - so the creative process of making the play a reality in performance continues.

5.5 THE TEMPEST IN THE THEATRE

When Prospero says to Miranda 'The fringed curtain of thine eye advance' (I.ii. 411) he is hopefully anticipating (in a perfect dramatic, iambic line) the moment when a curtain might draw aside to reveal Miranda and Ferdinand playing chess. It is a striking theatrical image and demonstrates how the *idea* of theatre permeates *The Tempest*. Some critics have suggested that this play is really a poem and others that it is too 'difficult' for an effective stage play. Such attitudes amount to a total failure to recognise the clues which every great dramatist gives to his would-be performers although *The Tempest* is certainly not an 'easy' play to perform well.

In the introductory sections of this book and in the Appendix there is an indication of the kind of theatrical conditions for which Shakespeare was writing. In addition, the play-text itself tells us a good deal about Shakespeare's ideas on presentation. We can see, for instance, the importance of good costumes: Prospero's magic garment; the hat and rapier which he wore as Duke of Milan; the clothes of the courtiers which, as Gonzalo remarks, have escaped damage from the sea; Caliban's 'gaberdine'; Trinculo's jester's outfit (Caliban calls him a 'pied ninny'!); Ariel's various disguises; the gaudy clothes which side-track Stephano and Trinculo and, of course, the elaborately costumed masque are all examples. Stage 'properties' are important too: Prospero's staff; the logs which Caliban and Ferdinand carry; Stephano's bottle and the 'line' which provides the puns and comic action for the clowns. *The Tempest* also suggests the use of ingenious stage machinery for the appearance and disappearance of the banquet and we know from sources contemporary with the play that in masques goddesses often made their entrances from above in clouds or aerial chariots controlled by wires and pulleys. The storm itself seems to require some scenic devices, possibly swaying rigging or lanterns and there are several instances in the play when a 'discovery space' or some inner recess is called for. Noises 'off-stage' such as the sound of the storm, the echoes in Ariel's songs, the sound of Prospero's 'hunting hounds' and so on, would sometimes have come from such a place if it were closed off.

Prospero refers to all such theatrical illusions in his speech after the masque (IV. i. 146–58). Every play is an 'insubstantial pageant' and the mention of

> The cloud-capped towers, the gorgeous palaces,
> The solemn temples, the great globe itself

is clearly intended to be ambiguous. The word 'rack' in the final line of the speech is the term used to describe a bank of stage clouds. At one level Shakespeare describes the scenic decorations of a masque and the word 'globe' is clearly an oblique reference to a famous theatre; at another these are man's futile attempt to construct something of permanence in a world which itself is only temporary.

However ephemeral the actors may be (and this is a favourite theme of Shakespeare's) the dramatist provides them with a great deal of solid 'business' in *The Tempest*. Such moments as the storm itself, Trinculo and Caliban under the gaberdine, Gonzalo's and Alonso's escape from near-death at the hands of Anthonio and Sebastian or Ariel's tricks on Trinculo and Stephano, all demonstrate a play *made* for performance.

Most of the events in the play are 'staged' by Prospero with Ariel as his stage-manager and chief performer – notice how Prospero praises Ariel's performance as a harpy following the 'mock banquet':

> Bravely the figure of this harpy hast thou
> Performed, my Ariel; a grace it had devouring. (III.iii. 83)

In this scene right through to his final appeal to the audience Prospero *becomes* the dramatist bringing his Art to a peak and then taking his leave of it.

After Shakespeare's death *The Tempest* suffered more than usually severe changes. In 1667 the poet and dramatist John Dryden (1631-1700) collaborated with the actor-manager Sir William Davenant (1606-1668) in rewriting the play, altering the plot and adding extra characters. This version held the stage until the late eighteenth century although in 1746 Charles Macklin (1700-97) and 1757 David Garrick (1717-79) both restored Shakespeare's version at Drury Lane. In Chapter 6 (on critical appraisals) you will find in both 6.1 and 6.2 many details of the play's reception and of the way it has been interpreted by actors and directors. The play has been turned into a pantomime, a puppet show (what Sebastian called 'A living drollery' (III.iii. 21)), several films and a television production. Many productions, notably Charles Kean's in 1857 have stressed the superb scenic possibilities of the play, yet Tyrone Guthrie's version in 1934 used little more than a log and some seaweed with equal success. There have been many intriguing Prosperos; Charles Laughton, Henry Ainley, Michael Redgrave, John Gielgud, Paul Scofield –all leading actors of their day; but the important actor-managers Frank Benson (in 1891) and Beerbohm Tree (in 1904) both opted to play Caliban. David Hirst's book *The Tempest: Text and Performance* gives many fascinating insights into recent productions and you should consult periodicals and newspapers for any current reviews.

There is no 'correct' way to perform *The Tempest* but you must engage in the imaginative reconstruction of it *as a play* if you are to make sense of the words on the page.

6 SPECIMEN PASSAGE
AND COMMENTARY

The following example shows the kind of close critical attention that is necessary for an analysis of part of the text. You cannot really claim to 'know' the play unless you have approached the entire text with this sort of care and to enable you to do this effectively I am suggesting a number of important stages in such an analysis.

First we must establish the *context* of the passage, understanding clearly the events that have given rise to the action covered by the extract being studied: in any examination answer, however, this must be stated *briefly*. Second, there must be an appreciation of *what is going on* both in terms of stage action and the psychological state of the various characters. Then we must turn specifically to the *language*, examining its style, content and the way in which it creates the dramatic effect such as atmosphere, tension, irony or climax. Initially we may need to ensure a complete understanding of obscure words or sentence structure and to be particularly wary of words that have changed their meaning since Shakespeare's day. For a proper appreciation of the content of a passage it may also be necessary to familiarise oneself with beliefs, attitudes and tastes of Elizabethan times, or with some contemporary event, and a good scholarly edition of the play should be particularly helpful in this respect. In the case of *The Tempest*, for example, some familiarity with Elizabethan courtly love-poetry – especially some sixteenth-century sonnets – will shed light on the expression of an idealised view of feminine beauty which Shakespeare utilises in this play. Above all we must remember this is a *play* we are considering, designed for performance in a theatre.

6.1 SPECIMEN PASSAGE

Act III, Scene ii, lines 108 to end of scene

STEPHANO Monster, I will kill this man; his daughter

and I will be King and Queen - save our Graces! -
and Trinculo and thyself shall be viceroys. Dost thou   110
like the plot, Trinculo?

TRINCULO Excellent.

STEPHANO Give me thy hand; I am sorry I beat thee;
but while thou livest keep a good tongue in thy head.

CALIBAN Within this half hour will he be asleep
Wilt thou destroy him then?

STEPHANO   Ay, on mine honour.

ARIEL [Aside] This will I tell my master.

CALIBAN Thou mak'st me merry; I am full of pleasure;
Let us be jocund. Will you troll the catch
You taught me but while-ere?   120

STEPHANO At thy request, monster, I will do reason, any
reason. Come on, Trinculo, let us sing.

He sings

Flout 'em and cout 'em
And scout 'em and flout 'em;
Thought is free.

CALIBAN That's not the tune.

ARIEL plays the tune on a tabor and pipe

STEPHANO What is this same?

TRINCULO This is the tune of our catch, played by the
picture of Nobody.

STEPHANO If thou beest a man, show thyself in thy   130
likeness. If thou beest a devil, take't as thou list.

TRINCULO O, forgive me my sins!

STEPHANO He that dies pays all debts. I defy thee.
Mercy upon us!

CALIBAN Art thou afeard?

STEPHANO No, monster, not I.

CALIBAN Be not afeard; the isle is full of noises,
Sounds and sweet airs, that give delight and hurt not.
Sometimes a thousand twangling instruments
Will hum about mine ears; and sometimes voices,   140
That if I then had waked after long sleep,
Will make me sleep again; and then, in dreaming,
The clouds methought would open, and show riches
Ready to drop upon me, that when I waked
I cried to dream again.

> STEPHANO This will prove a brave kingdom to me,
> where I shall have my music for nothing.
> CALIBAN When Prospero is destroyed.
> STEPHANO That shall be by and by: I remember the
> story.   150
> TRINCULO The sound is going away; let's follow it,
> and after do our work.
> STEPHANO Lead, monster, we'll follow. I would I could
> see this taborer, he lays it on.
> TRINCULO Wilt come? I'll follow Stephano. [*Exeunt*]

6.2 COMMENTARY

Stephano, Trinculo and Caliban have been drinking heavily and, watched by an unseen Ariel, Caliban has been attempting to provide further enticement for Stephano to kill Prospero. Caliban's efforts had been frustrated by Ariel whose interruptions had been mistaken for Trinculo's, but after Trinculo's beating Caliban has succeeded in tempting Stephano with Prospero's power and the beauty of Miranda.

At the opening of this extract Stephano, forgetting his dispute with Trinculo, announces, with characteristic self-importance, his intention of making the island his kingdom. This comic version of a usurpation of Prospero continues the theme which includes Prospero's usurpation by Anthonio, Prospero's occupation of Caliban's island and the plot for Sebastian to supplant Alonso. There is already a marked distinction between the intentions of Stephano, voiced unconvincingly in prose, and the intensity of Caliban's wishes, spoken in verse. We see a brief reconciliation between Stephano and Trinculo, foreshadowing similar more important moments later in the play and Ariel comments directly to the audience making it clear that he will inform Prospero. This is vital to the further development of the plot as it is Prospero's recollection of the threat to his life which provides a startling end to the masque.

Caliban has already told Stephano that Prospero takes a siesta; it is during this sleep that they hope to destroy him. In celebration Caliban turns to song. Stephano and Trinculo have clearly taught him drinking-songs – in this case a round expressing total contempt for the rest of the world with the illusory obverse that 'Thought is free'. Stephano, however, cannot even get this right, so intoxicated is he with drink and imaginary power. Ariel, therefore, provides a potent reminder of the presence of Prospero's powerful magic in the form of music from an unseen source. Appropriately he plays it on the jester's traditional instruments of pipe and drum and it is sufficient to provoke another comic incident reminiscent of the first appearance of the clowns in the play. They may well attempt to hide as they, misinterpreting Prospero's 'white magic', think that they are haunted by devils.

At this point Caliban begins to see his 'gods' in their true light. Stephano makes a feeble attempt to appear defiant of the unseen power but is quickly unnerved. His claim to be unafraid is totally unconvincing but Caliban's extended speech on the qualities of sound in the island shifts the focus from him. The contrast between the base 'civilised' mortals and Caliban is at its sharpest here: Caliban reveals that there are some aspects of his character more appropriate to the 'noble savage' than to the 'thing of darkness' which Prospero makes him out to be. His mastery of his recently-acquired language is such that he evokes the sensation of music with a series of soft sibilants ('s' sounds) followed by the wonderful onomatopoeia 'twangling' and humming 'm' and 'n' sounds. The speech shows Caliban's sensitivity to the qualities of music and the imaginative response it creates although he is unable to define his visions precisely, as befits their dreamlike nature. The experience is something he has in common with Ferdinand and the courtiers.

Stephano's response is typically mundane and prosaic. The urgency to kill Prospero is already dissolving with Ariel's magic music. Once again the clowns will be side-tracked in spite of Caliban's strong reminder. The scene ends in tension, Caliban frustrated, Trinculo attempting to entice Caliban to follow Stephano in the direction of the music rather than in the direction of Prospero's cell. The failure of the scene to come to any definite resolution means that its interest is continued into further scenes. Some of the play's themes however, have, been explored in a comic series of parallels to the central plot.

7 CRITICAL APPRAISALS

Actors and directors tend, quite understandably, to regard critics with suspicion because they know that adverse criticism can seriously damage the success of a production and that sometimes theatre critics have a power out of all proportion to their actual knowledge of the theatre. Students, similarly, ought to be wary of the other kind of critic - the literary critic who publishes books and essays about plays - for we must always remember that simply because something is in print, it is not necessarily to be accepted without question. Both sorts of critic, however objective they try to be, reveal something of their own prejudices and reflect the beliefs and values of their day and subsequent scholarship may sometimes prove them wrong. However, the work of experienced critics who have given careful attention to a play or its production can be extremely valuable to students in providing fresh insights and opinions backed up by evidence from the text or from the conditions surrounding the play's composition.

The Tempest has provoked very conflicting reactions from critics and for many years judgement of the play was complicated by the existence of the 'modified' versions, such as that by Dryden. Nevertheless, it has retained its popularity: it has had frequent productions and been the subject of many critical essays in this century. It is often regarded as the most elusive of Shakespeare's plays, and it is no wonder, therefore, that it has provoked so much wide and varied comment. This chapter contains a small sample of such responses: first, there are general comments concerning the nature of part or all of the play; and second, some critical responses to the play in performance. These short quotations from longer pieces are *not* intended for learning by heart, although some are indeed memorable; they are intended as a starting-point for your own thoughts and discussions; you are not expected to agree with them all or to accept the opinions expressed, but, remember, if you *disagree* you must back up your opinion with evidence from the play itself. You should particularly note the changes in style and content of the literary criticisms in different periods and the occasions when a production clearly achieved aspects of the playwright's intentions and when it obviously failed to do so!

7.1 GENERAL CRITICISMS OF THE PLAY

It seems to be as perfect of its kind, as almost anything we have of his. One may observe, that the Unities are kept here with an Exactness uncommon to the Liberties of his writings ... His Magick has something in it very Solemn and very Poetical: And that extravagant Character of *Caliban* is mighty well sustained, shews a wonderful Invention in the Author, who could strike out such a particular wild Image, and is certainly one of the finest and most uncommon Grotesques that was ever seen. (Nicholas Rowe 1709)

Of all the plays of Shakespeare, *The Tempest* is the most striking instance of his creative power. He has given the reins to his boundless imagination, and has carried the romantic, the wonderful, and the wild, to the most pleasing extravagance. The scene is a desolate island; and the characters the most new and singular that can be conceived: a prince who practises magic, an attendant spirit, a monster the son of a witch, and a young lady who has been brought to this solitude in her infancy, and had never beheld a man except her father. (Joseph Warton 1753)

Shakespeare seems to be the only poet who possesses the power of writing poetry with propriety of character; of which I know not an instance more striking than the image Calyban makes use of to express silence, which is at once highly poetical, and exactly suited to the wildness of the speaker:

> Pray you tread softly, that the blind mole may not
> Hear a foot-fall (Joseph Warton 1753)

The Tempest addresses itself entirely to the imaginative faculty: and although the illusion may be assisted by the effect on the senses of the complicated scenery and decorations of modern times yet this art of assistance is dangerous. For the principal and only genuine excitement ought to come from within. (S. T. Coleridge 1836)

Prospero has entered into complete possession of himself. Shakespeare has shown us his quick sense of injury, his intellectual impatience, his occasional moment of keen irritability, in order that we may be more deeply aware of his abiding strength and self possession, and that we may perceive how these have been grafted upon a temperament, not impassive or unexcitable. (Edward Dowden 1875)

The 'story' in *The Tempest* is a thing of naught. (Henry James 1907)

The Island is a realm where God is Good, where true Reason rules; it is what would be if Humanity – the best in man – controlled the life of man. (J. Middleton Murry 1936)

When we turn to Shakespeare's handling of this story, we first admire that which all must admire, the enchantment wherein he clothes it, the poetic feeling wherewith he suffuses it. Magic and music meet in *The Tempest* and are so wedded that none can put them asunder. (Sir Arthur Quiller-Couch 1940)

Prospero, who controls this comprehensive Shakespearean world, automatically reflects Shakespeare himself. Like Hamlet, he arranges dramatic shows to rouse his sinning victims' conscience. (G. Wilson Knight 1947)

Is *The Tempest* a Christian play? It is surely a profoundly religious poem, and of a Christ-like spirit in its infinite tenderness, its all-embracing sense of pity, its conclusion of joyful atonement and forgiveness, so general that even Caliban begins to talk of 'grace'. But it is not in the least Christian from the theological standpoint; there is no word of God, not a hint of immortality. (John Dover Wilson 1950)

It is hard to pick a speech at random without coming on an expression that brings us by analogy into direct contact with elements that seem remote because of their place in the action or because of the type of experience they symbolise. (Reuben Brower 1952)

Prospero's Art controls Nature; it requires of the artist virtue and temperance if his experiment is to succeed; and it thus stands for the world of the better natures and its qualities. (Frank Kermode 1954)

The Tempest has two endings: a quiet evening on the island when Prospero forgives his enemies and the story returns to the point of departure; and Prospero's tragic monologue, spoken directly to the audience, a monologue out of time. (Jan Kott 1964)

The Tempest is the second shortest play in the whole canon, and it has the fewest scenes. Theatrically, however, it is one of the most spectacular. (Hallett Smith 1969)

the play, composed throughout so musically, with a lovely diaphenity of verse scarcely distinguishable from the beautifully textured prose (Bonamy Dobree 1969)

Prospero's magic, in any case, is an 'art' which includes, in fact largely consists of, music and drama. (Northrop Frye 1969)

The famous lines on the mutability of man's works and of Nature herself come between . . . two assertions of Prospero's power. (Clifford Leech 1969)

The experiences they undergo on the island are felt by them to be strange, wonderful, unnatural - these are words that echo throughout the play. (A. C. and J. E. Spearing 1971)

what now awaits the conspirators is 'lingering perdition' from which nothing can deliver them but 'heart sorrow/And a clear life ensuing'. Here is the Christian doctrine of contrition defined in four words, and no theologian could have put it better. (Robert Speaight 1976)

The Tempest, one of the masterpieces of all literature, is also the most enigmatic of Shakespeare's works, and can be theatrically unsatisfying. A great deal of its substance seems deliberately hidden beneath the surface. (John Goodwin 1979)

The elders find what they have lost, though they have been transformed by the experience of loss and grief. Taught by suffering, they make a better way clear for those coming after to suceed them. (Judith Cook 1983)

The Tempest is a play about power. (David Hirst 1984)

You may wish to use many of these statements as a basis for your revision; clearly you must check many of them against the text and you should ensure that you have understood such concepts as 'mutability' - the idea of change through time - and the various doctrinal points raised by critics.

7.2 THEATRE CRITICISMS

One of the most strikingly original conceptions was the entire execution of the music (with the exception of the duet in the masque) by an invisible choir, led by Miss Poole, whose mellow voice sounded with the rich, full clearness of a bell . . . we were really presented with a 'delicate spirit'. Ariel, at one moment, descending in a ball of fire; at another rising gently from a tuft of flowers; again sailing on the smooth waters on the back of a dolphin; then gliding noiselessly over the sands, as a water nymph. (John William Cole on Charles Kean's production, (1857)

My contention is that unless *The Tempest* be produced in such a way as to bring home to audiences the fantasy and beauty of the play it were better not to attempt it at all. (Herbert Beerbohm Tree defending his own production, 1904)

Caliban, played by the actor-manager, was so grand and grotesque that he swamped the lovers and Prospero alike. The epilogue was cut and the play ended with a vision of the ship sailing away leaving Caliban firmly centre-stage shading his eyes to catch a final glimpse of the boat transporting a civilisation he humbly worshipped. (*The Times* on Tree's production, 1904)

Prospero, who is usually made into a dull old boy by most actors, in John's sensitive hands became a being of great beauty. (Harcourt Williams on Gielgud's performance, 1930)

He who impersonates Prospero impersonates also the creator of Prospero. (Max Beerbohm 1932)

Mr Ainley played the old codger (Prospero) like a toast master celebrating his golden wedding; while another famous actor reminded me of a conjuror in decreasing demand at Masonic Banquets . . . Mr Laughton, by the aid of taking thought and some first-class wiggery, composed a Prospero derivative snowily from Blake, Devrient's Lear, Noe, possibly Noah himself and certainly Father Christmas. (James Agate 1943)

Apart from the drama of the storm there is little enough action – not so much unwinding of a plot as the unravelling of the spell cast by Prospero. Audibility, then, is the first requirement and a magical touch the second. Alan Judd, though not always suggesting that he controlled the destinies of men and spirits, brought a ringing voice to the part of Prospero. Robert Atkins, looking like the incarnation of Palaeolithic Man, was a credible Caliban and Michael Picardie's fleet-footedness and trapped bird gestures cleverly suggested Ariel. (Helen Wicks at the Open Air Production in Regents Park, 1960)

As to the suitability of Michael Tippett's music for an Ariel who was primarily an actor to sing, the dubious results, I fear, must stand. (Caryl Brahms on the Old Vic production, 1962)

The low comedy . . . is given with an unusually uninhibited gusto. David Warner's galumping string bean Trinculo and Derek Smith's blazing strutting little cockatoo of a Stephano go at their knock-about business with a relish. . . This is good stuff, it clothes Shakespeare's images with flesh. Caliban, too, is indeed 'a thing most brutish' – black as sin, most horribly swollen with sores, loathsome with tufts of hair, priapic and gluttonous. (John Perceval on the Stratford production, 1963)

You can rationalise until you are blue in the face about the themes of the play, about forgiveness and reconciliation, about reality and illusion. Unless these ideas are conveyed as concrete meaning in the theatre, the play does not work. (John Perceval, Stratford, 1962)

Traditionally *The Tempest* is one of the hardest of all Shakespeare's plays to produce. Since it is clear from the start of the second scene that Prospero holds all the cards, dramatic conflict is virtually non-existent. What I looked for . . . and rather missed, was a strong interpretative thread that would help to turn what is essentially a dramatic poem into a play (Michael Billington on the Chichester production, 1968)

I've seen more visually seductive *Tempests* but never one with a stronger governing idea . . . that Prospero has arrogated to himself the godlike power of the instinctive colonist and that he must renounce his morally unjustified authority before he can again become a part of a civilised, ordered, society. I don't mind the absence of a realistic Hollywood-style storm, nor do I care greatly about the omission of the masque . . . usually more reminiscent of a Number Three tour of *Oklahoma* than a dignified, pagan ritual. (Michael Billington on Jonathan Miller's production, 1970)

At the centre of the brilliant masque ... there is a harmonious vision of order – but controlled by a Juno who closely resembles the dead Queen Elizabeth, suggesting a measure of nostalgia in Prospero's hierarchical dreaming. . . After circling his enemies (in the final scene) . . . Prospero finally grants them redemption – but he noticeably fails to greet his brother Anthonio. In the final moment, the two brothers confront each other in silence, dressed in . . . identical costumes – clearly their conflict remains unresolved. (Peter Ansorge on the National Theatre production, 1974)

One of the keys to making this play work for an audience today is to find a modern equivalent for Prospero's magical powers, acceptable enough in Jacobean times but remote from our rational and determinist age. (Jonathan Hammond on the Wyndham's production, 1975)

The masque . . . is a very different affair from that Shakespeare envisaged . . . the director's politics – here his sexual politics – transform Shakespeare's presentation of a celebratory masque which crumbles at the onset of reality into a modern statement on the difficulty of believing that marriage is an institution which inspires absolute faith. (David Hirst on Derek Jarman's 1980 film of *The Tempest*)

But the production which has worked best for me, and which managed to achieve the right balance – where poetry, fantasy, pageantry and humour came together as they should – was that of Ron Daniels for the Royal Shakespeare Company at Stratford in 1982 (Judith Cook, 1983)

You are strongly advised to study these statements carefully because of the very interesting and vital issues they raise. Your attention is particularly drawn to John Perceval's comment (1962) concerning the importance of converting the play's themes to 'concrete meaning' in the theatre. This is usually dependent on the director's having a strong 'governing idea' (see 1970) but clearly this must be rooted in the *playwright's* ideas. These comments demonstrate a wide range of opinions – many of which you may wish to challenge – but they all convey something of the difficulty of presenting this play in the theatre. However, to describe it as a 'theatrical poem' simply because it is notoriously difficult is to evade the issue. Difficulty should not be confused with impossibility and the vast range of possible interpretations of the play is what makes it as fascinating now as when it was written.

REVISION QUESTIONS
AND SUGGESTIONS

1. How does *The Tempest* explore the concepts of illusion and reality?

2. To what extent is the idea of reconciliation a dominant theme in *The Tempest*? How does Shakespeare ensure that this theme is made dramatically effective?

3. Discuss either 'theatre' or 'music' as agents of Prospero's magic.

4. How does *The Tempest* relate to its likely sources?

5. Trace the idea of colonisation in the play.

6. What is Prospero's project and to what extent are the ends achieved?

7. How are the themes of fruitfulness and abundance presented in the masque?

8. Discuss the nature of the relationship between (a) Prospero and Miranda; (b) Miranda and Ferdinand; (c) Prospero and Ariel.

9. What purpose do the 'clowns' serve in *The Tempest*?

10. Examine Shakespeare's use of dramatic verse in *The Tempest*. How does it reveal a mature playwright at work?

11. Why is *The Tempest* a particularly difficult play to present satisfactorily in the theatre?

12. What role is played by the sea in the action and ideas of *The Tempest*?

13. Consider in detail the idea that *The Tempest* is a Christian allegory.

14. With reference to Gonzalo's speech (V. i. 205-13) explain how the ideas of 'lost' and 'found' provide an important level of interpretation in *The Tempest*.

APPENDIX:
SHAKESPEARE'S THEATRE

We should speak, as Murel Bradbrook reminds us, not of the Elizabethan stage but of Elizabethan stages. Plays of Shakespeare were acted on tour, in the halls of mansions, one at least in Gray's Inn, frequently at Court, and after 1609 at the Blackfriars, a small, roofed theatre for those who could afford the price. But even after his Company acquired the Blackfriars, we know of no play of his not acted (unless, rather improbably, *Troilus* is an exception) for the general public at the Globe, or before 1599 at its predecessor, the Theatre, which, since the Globe was constructed from the same timbers, must have resembled it. Describing the Globe, we can claim therefore to be describing, in an acceptable sense, Shakespeare's theatre, the physical structure his plays were designed to fit. Even in the few probably written for a first performance elsewhere, adaptability to that structure would be in his mind.

For the facilities of the Globe we have evidence from the drawing of the Swan theatre (based on a sketch made by a visitor to London about 1596) which depicts the interior of another public theatre; the builder's contract for the Fortune theatre, which in certain respects (fortunately including the dimensions and position of the stage) was to copy the Globe; indications in the dramatic texts; comments, like Ben Jonson's on the throne let down from above by machinery; and eye-witness testimony to the number of spectators (in round figures, 3000) accommodated in the auditorium.

In communicating with the audience, the actor was most favourably placed. Soliloquising at the centre of the front of the great platform, he was at the mid-point of the theatre, with no one among the spectators more than sixty feet away from him. That platform-stage (Figs I and II) was the most important feature for performance at the Globe. It had the audience – standing in the yard (10) and seated in the galleries (9) – on three sides of it. It was 43 feet wide, and 27½ feet from front to back. Raised (?5½ feet) above the level of the yard, it had a trap-door (II.8)

SHAKESPEARE'S THEATRE

The stage and its adjuncts; the tiring-house; and the auditorium.

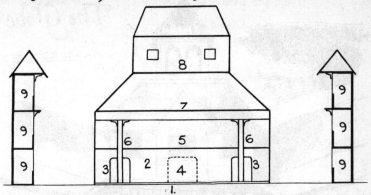

FIG I ELEVATION

1. Platform stage (approximately five feet above the ground) 2. Tiring-house
3. Tiring-house doors to stage 4. Conjectured third door 5. Tiring-house
gallery (balustrade and partitioning not shown) 6. Pillars supporting the
heavens 7. The heavens 8. The hut 9. The spectators' galleries

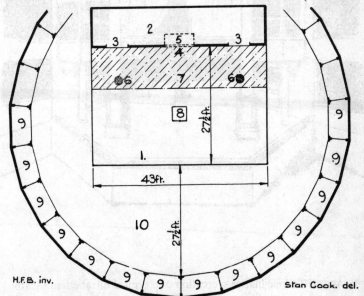

H.F.B. inv.   Stan Cook. del.

FIG II PLAN

1. Platform stage 2. Tiring-house 3. Tiring-house doors to stage
4. Conjectural third door 5. Conjectural discovery space (alternatively behind 3)
6. Pillars supporting the heavens 7. The heavens 8. Trap door 9. Spectators'
gallery 10. The yard

The Globe

An artist's imaginative recreation of a typical Elizabethan theatre

giving access to the space below it. The actors, with their equipment, occupied the 'tiring house' (attiring-house: 2) immediately at the back of the stage. The stage-direction 'within' means inside the tiring-house. Along its frontage, probably from the top of the second storey, juts out the canopy or 'Heavens', carried on two large pillars rising through the platform (6, 7) and sheltering the rear part of the stage, the rest of which, like the yard, was open to the sky. If the 'hut' (I.8), housing the machinery for descents, stood, as in the Swan drawing, above the 'Heavens', that covering must have had a trap-door, so that the descents could be made through it.

Descents are one illustration of the vertical dimension the dramatist could use to supplement the playing-area of the great platform. The other opportunities are provided by the tiring-house frontage or facade. About this facade the evidence is not as complete or clear as we should like, so that Fig. I is in part conjectural. Two doors giving entry to the platform there certainly were (3). A third (4) is probable but not certain. When curtained, a door, most probably this one, would furnish what must be termed a discovery-space (II.5), not an inner stage (on which action in any depth would have been out of sight for a significant part of the audience). Usually no more than two actors were revealed (exceptionally, three), who often then moved out on to the platform. An example of this is Ferdinand and Miranda in *The Tempest* 'discovered' at chess, then seen on the platform speaking with their fathers. Similarly the gallery (I.5) was not an upper stage. Its use was not limited to the actors: sometimes it functioned as 'lords' rooms' for favoured spectators, sometimes, perhaps, as a musician's gallery. Frequently the whole gallery would not be needed for what took place aloft: a window-stage (as in the first balcony scene in *Romeo*, even perhaps in the second) would suffice. Most probably this would be a part (at one end) of the gallery itself; or just possibly, if the gallery did not (as it does in the Swan drawing) extend the whole width of the tiring-house, a window over the left or right-hand door. As the texts show, whatever was presented aloft, or in the discovery-space, was directly related to the action on the platform, so that at no time was there left, between the audience and the action of the drama, a great bare space of platform-stage. In relating Shakespeare's drama to the physical conditions of the theatre, the primacy of that platform is never to be forgotten.

Note: The present brief account owes most to C. Walter Hodges, *The Globe Restored*; Richard Hosley in *A New Companion to Shakespeare Studies*, and in *The Revels History of English Drama*; and to articles by Hosley and Richard Southern in *Shakespeare Survey*, 12, 1959, where full discussion can be found.

HAROLD BROOKS

FURTHER READING

Shakespeare's life and work as a playwright

Reese, M.M., *Shakespeare, His World and his Work* (London: Arnold, 1980)

Speaight, Robert, *Shakespeare, The Man and his Achievement* (London: Dent, 1977).

For problems concerned in studying plays

Bradby, D. Thomas, P. and Pickering, K., *Studying Drama* (London: Croom Helm, 1983).

Peck, John and Coyle, Martin, *Literary Terms and Criticism* (London: Macmillan, 1984); *How to Study a Shakespeare Play* (London: Macmillan, 1985).

Further discussion on issues raised in this study

Clemen, Wolfgang, *The Development of Shakespeare's Imagery* (London: Methuen, 1977).

Cook, Judith, *Shakespeare's Players* (London: Harrap, 1983).

Hirst, David, *The Tempest: Text and Performance* (London: Macmillan, 1984).

Hunt, John Dixon, *The Tempest* (London: Macmillan, 1982).

Palmer, D.J., *The Tempest – Casebook* (London: Macmillan, 1968).